A Time ...

Peggy Williams

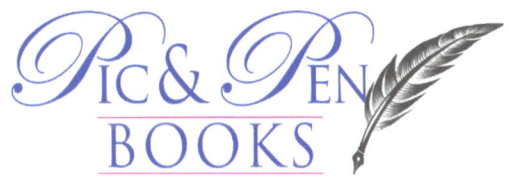

OMAHA, NEBRASKA

ISBN: 978-09824294-5-7

LCCN: 2019915177

Library of Congress data on file with the Publisher

Pic & Pen Books, Omaha, NE

Design and production by Concierge Marketing Inc.

Scripture quotations marked NKJV are taken from the New King James Version®. Copyright © 1982 by Thomas Nelson. Used by permission. All rights reserved.

Scripture quotations marked NIV are taken from the Holy Bible, New International Version®, NIV®. Copyright © 1973, 1978, 1984, 2011 by Biblica, Inc.® Used by permission of Zondervan. All rights reserved worldwide. www.zondervan.com. The "NIV" and "New International Version" are trademarks registered in the United States Patent and Trademark Office by Biblica, Inc.®
Publisher of this book has capitalized certain references to deity that are not shown capitalized in this Bible version, but for consistency in the published work.

Scripture quotations marked NASB are taken from the New American Standard Bible®. Copyright © 1960, 1962, 1963, 1968, 1971, 1972, 1973, 1975, 1977, 1995 by The Lockman Foundation. Used by permission. www.lockman.org.

PRINTED IN THE UNITED STATES OF AMERICA

10 9 8 7 6 5 4 3 2 1

This book is created in loving memory of
Ida and her treasured faith of which she often spoke.

The blossoming cactus on the front cover of this book
attests to her love for family and plants. She passed from this life
without seeing a time for this particular cactus blossom.
She would have smiled if she had seen its beauty.

Introduction

Ida's cactus reveals a stunning pink blossom which appeared 17 years after her passing. Her grandchildren lovingly cared for this cactus (after she passed) and were pleasantly surprised to see its lovely flower appear when least expected after all this time.

Imagine, if you will, God's smile revealed in beauty on this earth—in this case, a stunning cactus blossom.

With the exception of the cactus flower photographs on the cover and pages 42–44 and 46, taken by S.B., all other photos were taken by this author. Thank you, S.B.

I thank my husband for his patience and valuable input, Lisa for her expertise and creativity, and my friends for guidance and encouragement.

Finally, all glory goes to God.

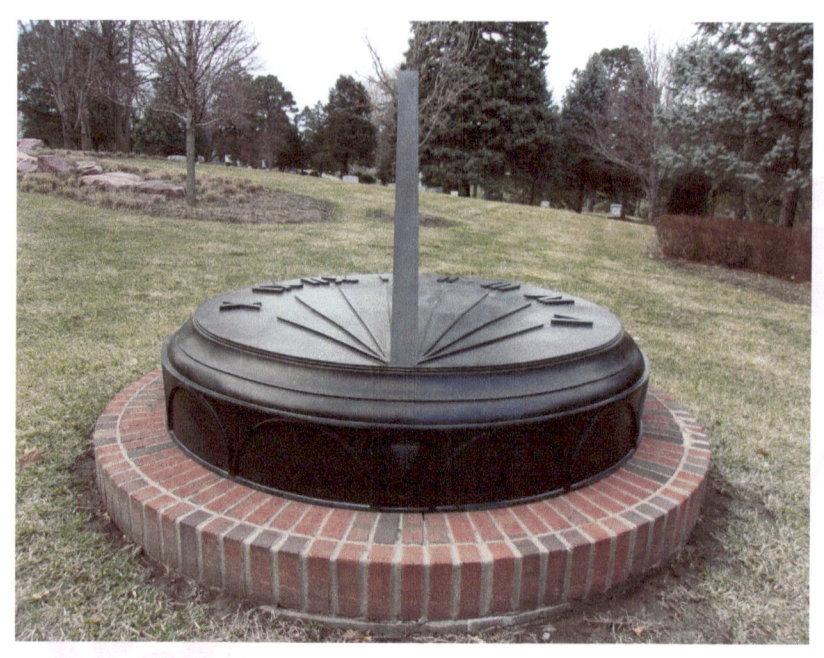

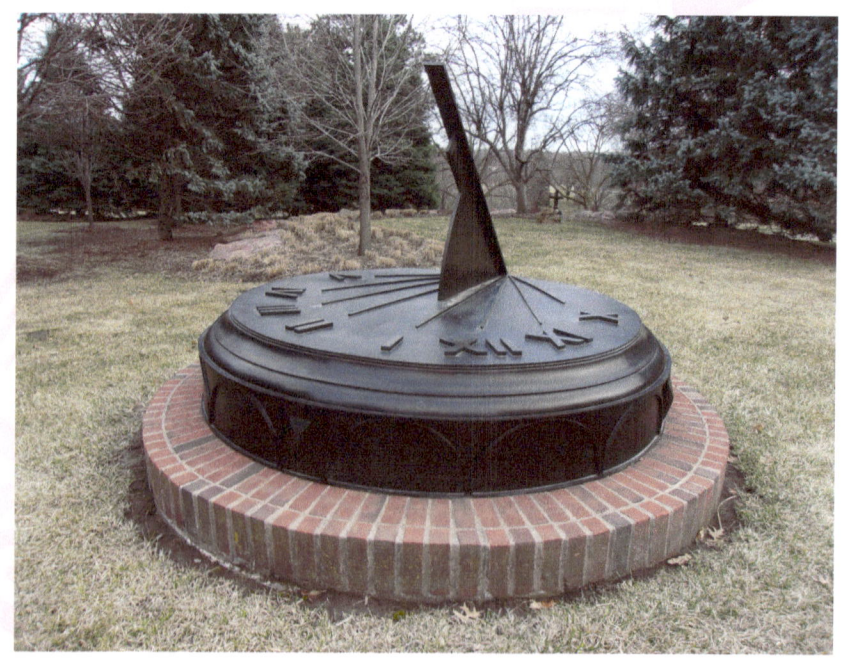

A Time...

For reflection. **_January_** ushers in the idea of beginning again! Motivation runs high. A new calendar year unfolds day by day–often impelling one to ponder fresh goals, ideas, projects, friends, and health incentives–to name a few. The fascinating aging process accompanies the passage of time. Webster's New Collegiate Dictionary gives one definition of the word **process** as: "a natural phenomenon marked by gradual changes that lead toward a particular result."[1]

Individuals living their lives to old age understand (from decade to decade) "gradual" changes to the body. Aches surface from seemingly nowhere. Motions and abilities take on challenging movements. Humility and submission creep into one's personality.

What does the Bible say about "old"?

"They shall still bear fruit in old age; they shall be fresh and flourishing"
(Psalm 92:14, NKJV).

"The silver-haired head is a crown of glory, if it is found in the way of righteousness"
(Proverbs 16:31, NKJV).

"Even to your old age and gray hairs I am He, I am He who will sustain you. I have made you and I will carry you; I will sustain you and I will rescue you"
(Isaiah 46:4, NIV).

"Since my youth, O God, You have taught me, and to this day I declare Your marvelous deeds. Even when I am old and gray, do not forsake me, O God, till I declare Your power to the next generation, Your might to all who are to come" *(Ps. 71:17-18, NIV).*

Questions about life, its purpose, its fragility, etc., often arise as one moves through the aging process. These questions are not new.

Job, a man from the Old Testament received disastrous news of the theft of his oxen and donkeys, and death of servants. That same day he received word that the fire of God fell from the sky and burned up the sheep and servants. Another messenger brought him news that his camels were carried off and servants put to death by raiding parties. If that were not enough, still another messenger informed him of the death of his sons and daughters as a result of the collapsed house in which they were feasting (Job 1:13-33).

Three of Job's friends came to him, and "they sat down with him on the ground seven days and seven nights, and no one spoke a word to him, for they saw that his grief was very great" (Job 2:13, NKJV).

Surely, during that seven-day period, Job thought much about life and God. Amazingly, these words were penned as coming from Job's mouth, "Naked I came from my mother's womb, and naked I will depart. The Lord gave and the Lord has taken away; may the name of the Lord be praised" (Job 1:21, NIV).

Some days are such that one wishes to begin again and have a fresh new morning. Unfortunately, a day lived cannot be "played back" anew from the morning or any part of that day until its ending.

One life only is allotted to each individual. "How to live" instructions are not humanly preprogrammed or set in stone for any individual. However, the Bible guides those who observe its words, which are the words of God.

"Be very careful, then, how you live—not as unwise but as wise, making the most of every opportunity,…" (Eph. 5:15-16, NIV).

Each new day dawns with time certain to be used—moment by moment. Ecclesiastes 3 summarizes time quite well.

"There is a time for everything, and a season for every activity under heaven: a time to be born and a time to die, a time to plant and a time to uproot, a time to kill and a time to heal, a time to tear down and a time to build, a time to weep and a time to laugh, a time to mourn and a time to dance, a time to scatter stones and a time to gather them, a time to embrace and a time to refrain, a time to search and a time to give up, a time to keep and a time to throw away, a time to tear and a time to mend, a time to be silent and a time to speak, a time to love and a time to hate, a time for war and a time for peace"
(Eccl. 3:1-8 NIV).

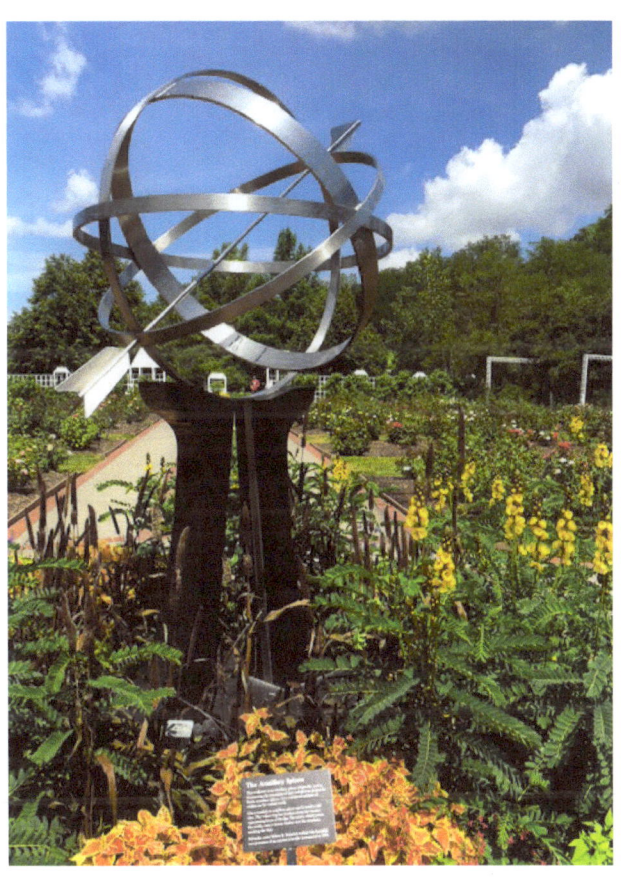

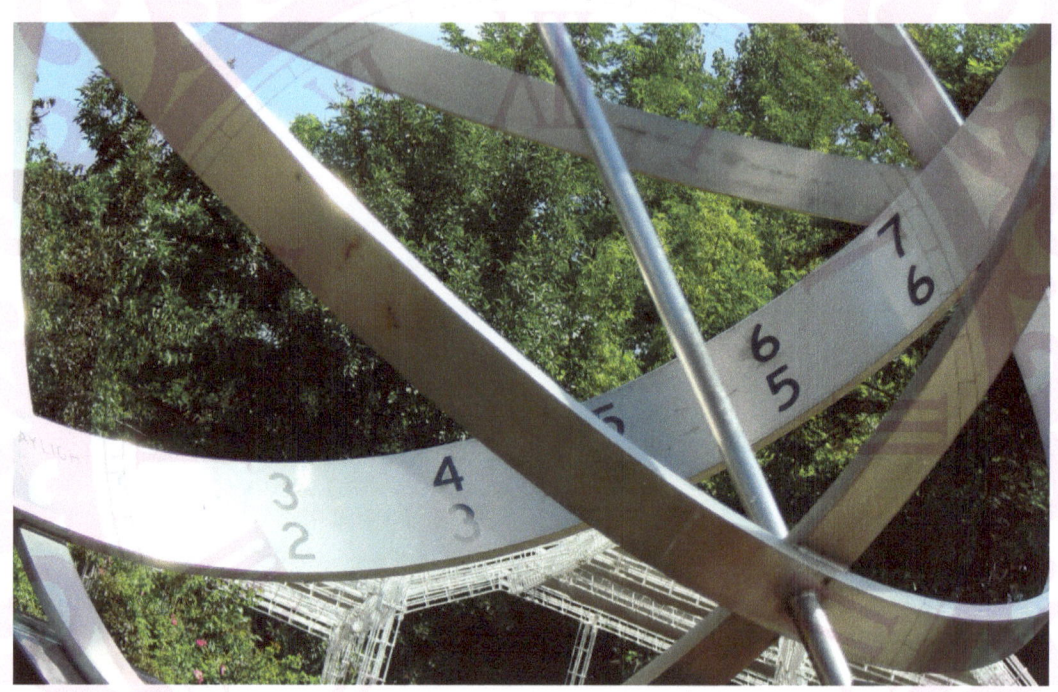

What is life without thinking of God who made life with a word (Genesis 1:26-27)? How precious is life! What a joy to have the opportunity to experience life. The Creator of all life is the giver of true joy. Breathe in the fresh spring air of this earth; feel the wind blow through your hair. Feel the rain on your face during a summer shower. Hear the laughter of another human being; see a smile come alive on the face of a loved one. Oh, to have one more day to enjoy God's beauty in this earth—the sun, the billowy white clouds, the blue sky.

Time passes so quickly! But there are moments remaining today. In spite of all that has transpired to this point, time is still available for a new heart, new joy, new thankfulness to God our Creator.

"After this, Job lived 140 years, and saw his sons and his grandsons, four generations. And Job died, an old man and full of days" (Job 42:16-17, NASB).

The Armillary Sphere

This sculpture is an armillary sphere. Originally used to demonstrate the movement of stars and planets around the Earth, armillary spheres were considered symbols of wisdom in the ancient world.

Like a sundial, an armillary sphere can be used to tell time. The widest ring has numbers along the interior representing hours of the day. The arrow, which points due north, casts a narrow shadow over the numbers, marking the time.

Nebraska artist Milton B. Heinrich crafted this beautiful interpretation of an ancient scientific instrument in 1995.

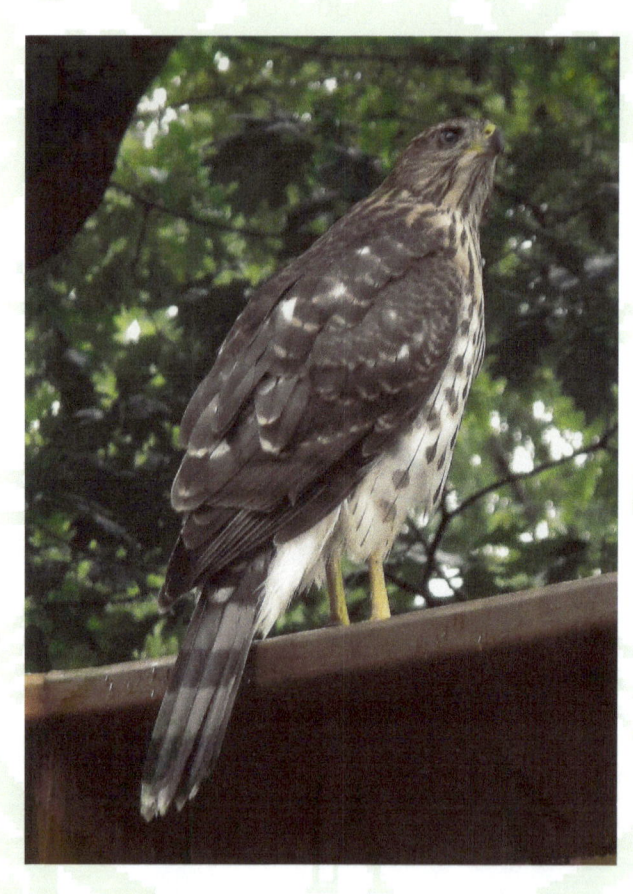

Reflect?

Yes—but resolve to live each moment to its fullest!!!

What a treasure to have been given life!

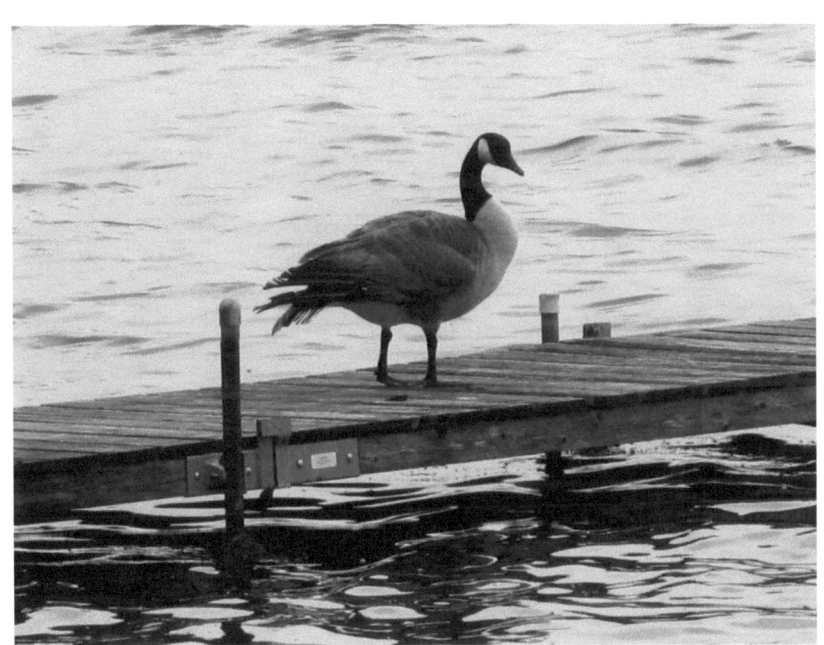

[1]Webster's New Collegiate Dictionary (Springfield, MA, 1980), 910.

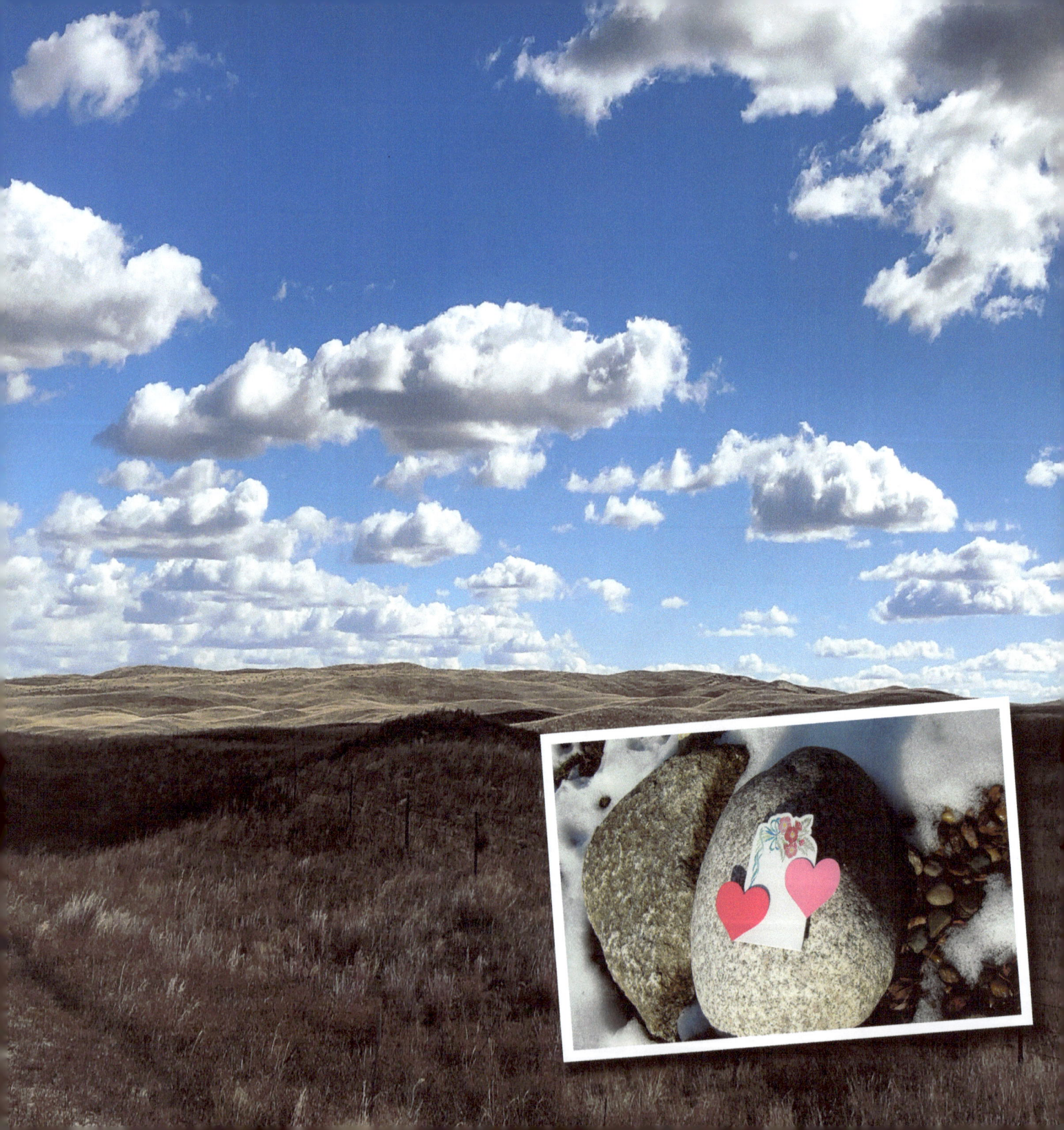

A Time ...

For observance. The calendar month of *February* reveals at least three holiday observances: Groundhog Day, Valentine's Day, and Presidents Day.

In America, Groundhog Day is observed February 2. Evolving from European animalism and nature worship thousands of years ago, popular culture today celebrates the appearance of a groundhog named Punxsutawney Phil from Gobbler's Knob near Punxsutawney, Pennsylvania[1]. In years past, the belief was that a badger could predict the coming of spring. Therefore, folks watched the badger in order to know when to plant crops.

Valentine's Day, observed February 14, seems to have connections to a dark and dismal past. No one knows the exact origin, but pagan rituals, fertility feast, and martyrdom practices predate this observance.[2] Chaucer and Shakespeare romanticized Valentine's Day in their work, and handmade paper cards marked the expression of love in the Middle Ages. In the 19th Century, factory-made cards replaced these handmade paper cards.

In regard to Presidents Day in America, two notable presidents' birthdays are recognized: Abraham Lincoln (February 12) and George Washington (February 22). In 1971, President Richard Nixon proclaimed one single federal public holiday, and called it Presidents Day.[3] Each year this holiday is observed the third Monday in February and honors all past presidents of the United States of America.

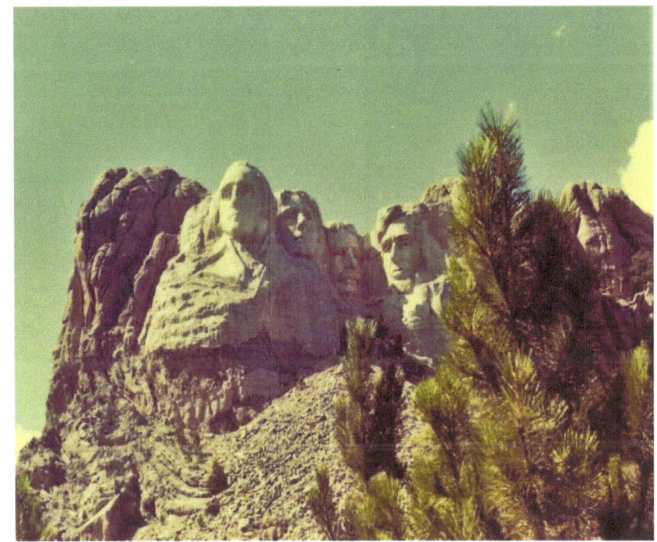

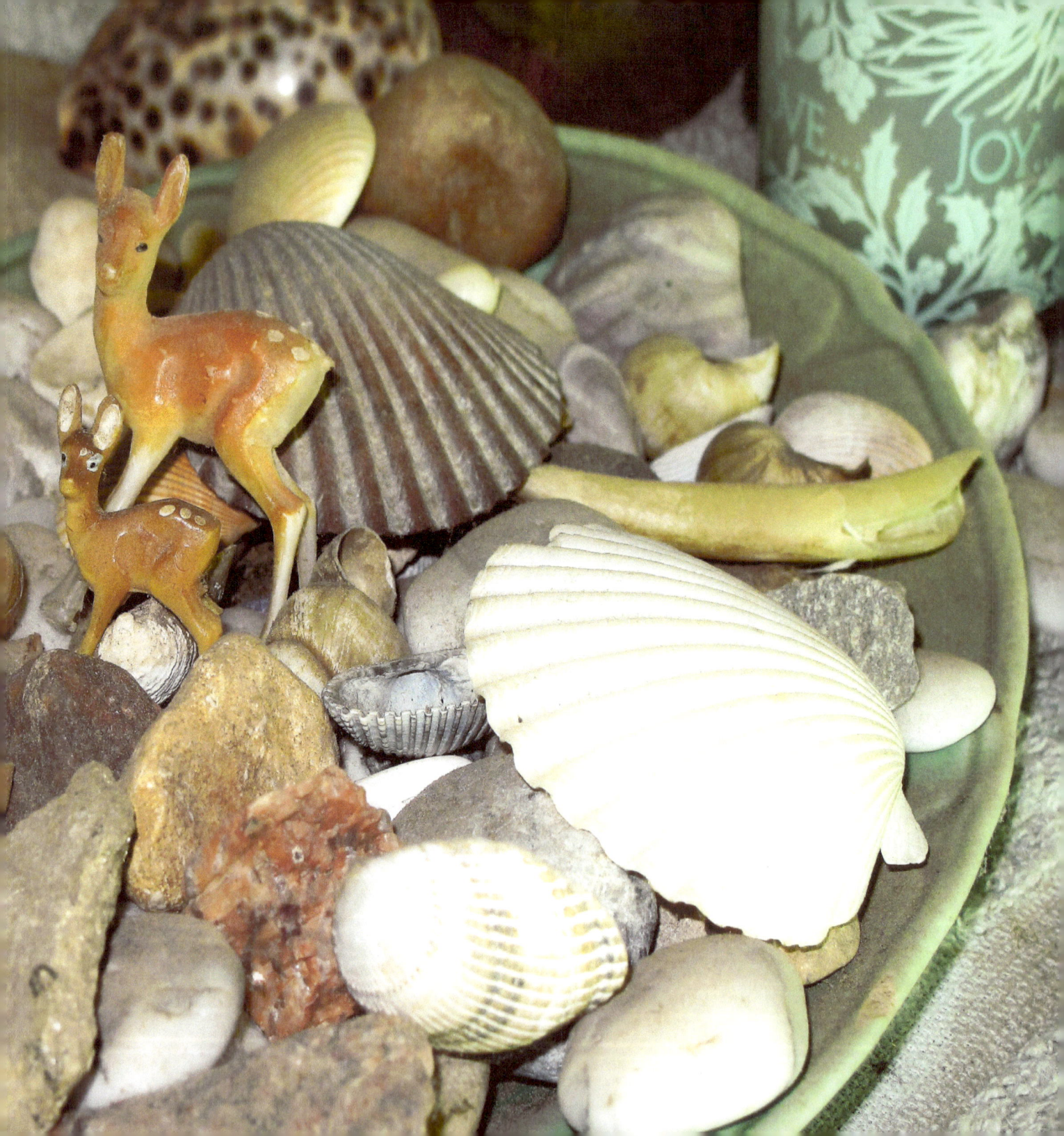

Could these observances be a result of the human heart yearning for something? Groundhog Day may be a search for signs to show the way of the future. Valentine's Day presents the opportunity to visibly express emotion to someone deemed near and dear. Presidents Day may help to fill the heartache from the loss of a loved one by positively remembering past historical figures.

If our hearts yearn to know the future, thirst for that deep loving relationship, or ache for the return to happy times from the past, one answer fulfills these longings. That answer is **Jesus Christ**, "the same yesterday and today and forever" (Hebrews 13:8, NIV). Jesus teaches that fulfillment is found in Him alone.

> *"And Jesus said to them, 'I am the bread of life. He who comes to Me shall never hunger, and he who believes in Me shall never thirst'"*
> *(John 6:35, NKJV).*

> *"For He satisfies the longing soul, and fills the hungry soul with goodness"*
> *(Psalm 107:9, NKJV).*

God our Savior desires that all be saved (1 Timothy 2:4). His desire will be fulfillment of yearnings for all believers. Observe, and take action. Spread the love of a Savior who cares.

1 www.timeanddate.com/holidays/us/groundhog-day.
2 www.npr.org/2011/02/14/133693152/the-dark-origins-of-valentines-day.
3 www.usafederalholidays.com/presidents-day/.

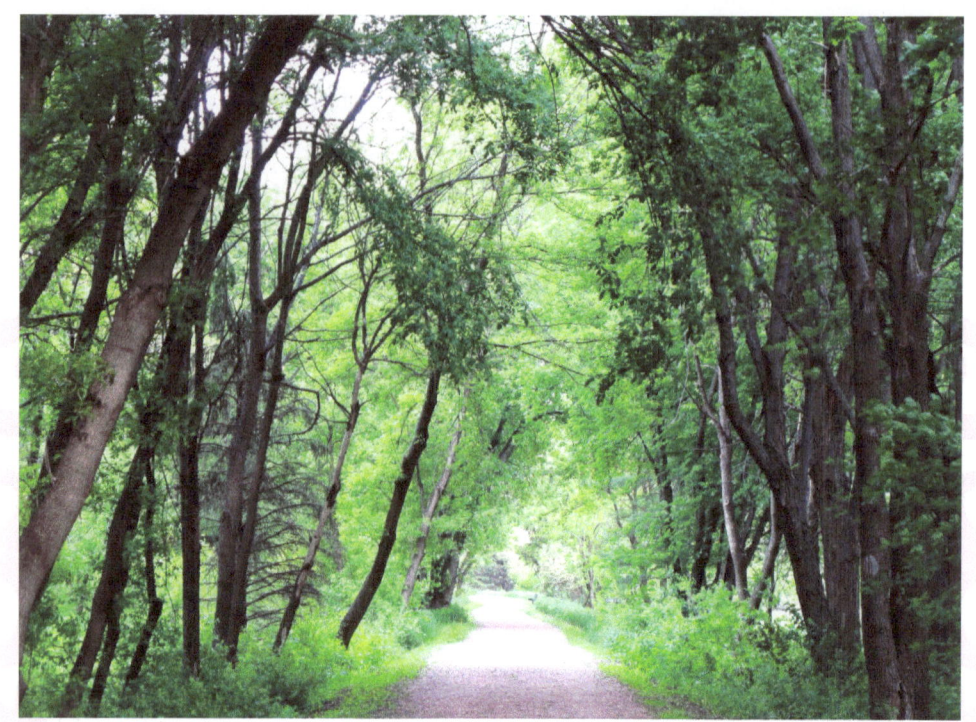

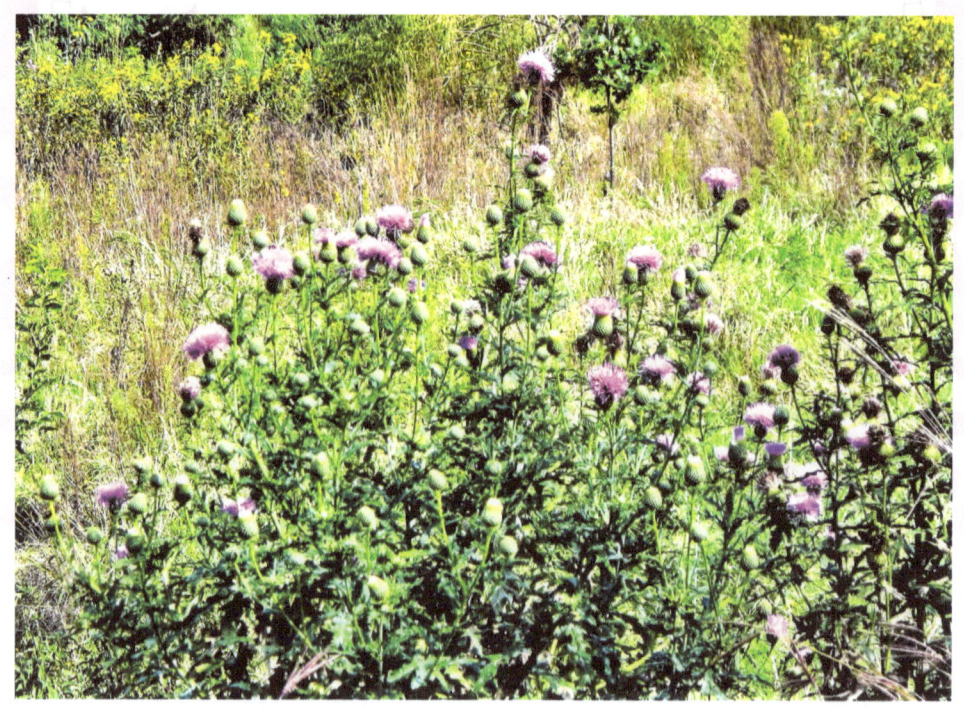

A Time ...

For newness. The month of ***March*** ushers in a new season—Spring. Time jumps forward an hour as a result of Daylight Savings Time. The Irish holiday, Saint Patrick's Day, appears on the calendar in March, and the color green again appears prevalent not only for that holiday, but also in grass and tree foliage.

But ponder for a moment. In life, how does one begin a new season? Certain landmarks help identify a new season: graduation from high school or college; employment in a new job; marriage, as well as the birth of that first child.

When one's life has experienced several decades, how is it possible to begin a new season? Many decisions have been made (positive or negative), pushing one further and further on a one-way path forward. There is no turning back; changing paths to the right or left are not options. How may one divert from the present course and begin a new season in life?

Jesus faced a myriad of decision-making opportunities during His time on earth. In Mark 6:3 He is referenced as a carpenter. Several times He is referred to as a teacher (Mark 4:38, Mark 10:17, John 3:2). He healed many who were sick. His mission on earth, however, was very specific. Jesus' unaltered focus was to do the will of His heavenly Father. Jesus never deviated from His task of the Gospel message. He talked to those who listened. He addressed individuals, special groups (disciples), and large crowds. His listeners came from all walks of life and ranged from young to the old (Matthew 18:1-5; John 8:7-9). Jesus remained focused on His heavenly Father and kept in touch through prayer (Luke 11:1-13).

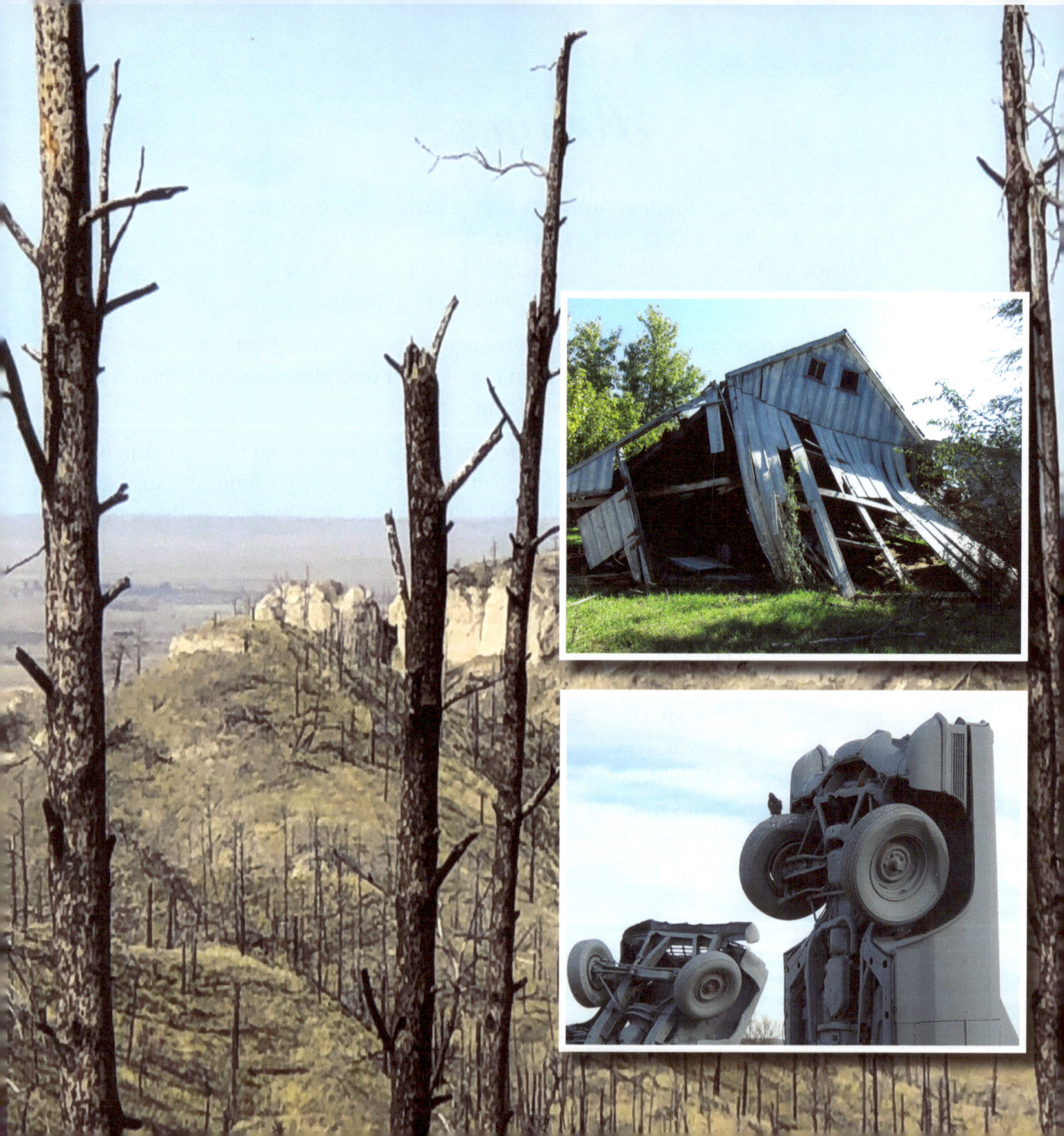

Jesus talked the talk perfectly, and walked the walk perfectly to fulfill the mission for His life. Because of sin, humans cannot follow Jesus' perfect life. So how does one begin a new season in a "weathered" life? Various Bible passages give guidance.

"For nothing will be impossible with God" (Luke 1:37, NASB).

"For we are His workmanship, created in Christ Jesus for good works, which God prepared beforehand that we should walk in them" (Ephesians 2:10, NKJV).

"Do not conform any longer to the pattern of this world, but be transformed by the renewing of your mind. Then you will be able to test and approve what God's will is—His good, pleasing and perfect will" (Romans 12:2, NIV).

"Therefore if anyone is in Christ, he is a new creature; the old things passed away; behold, new things have come"

(2 Corinthians 5:17, NASB).

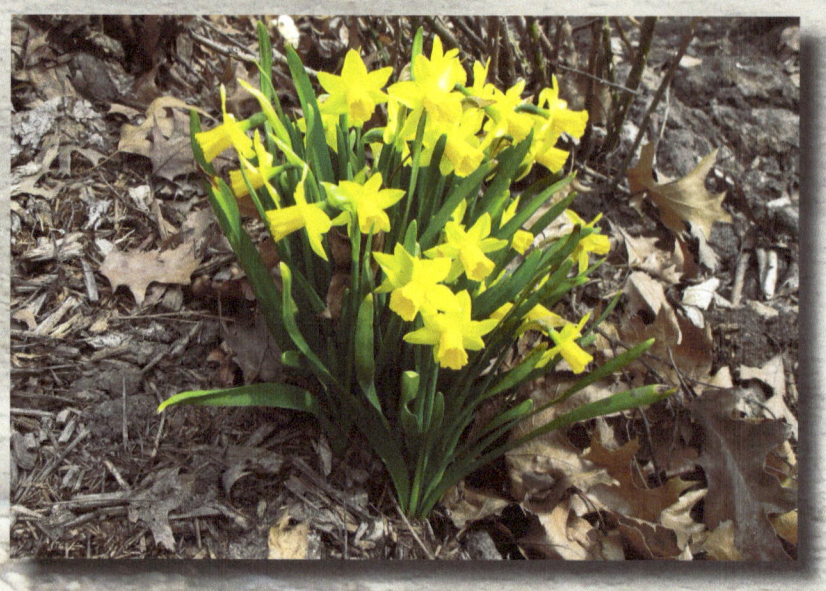

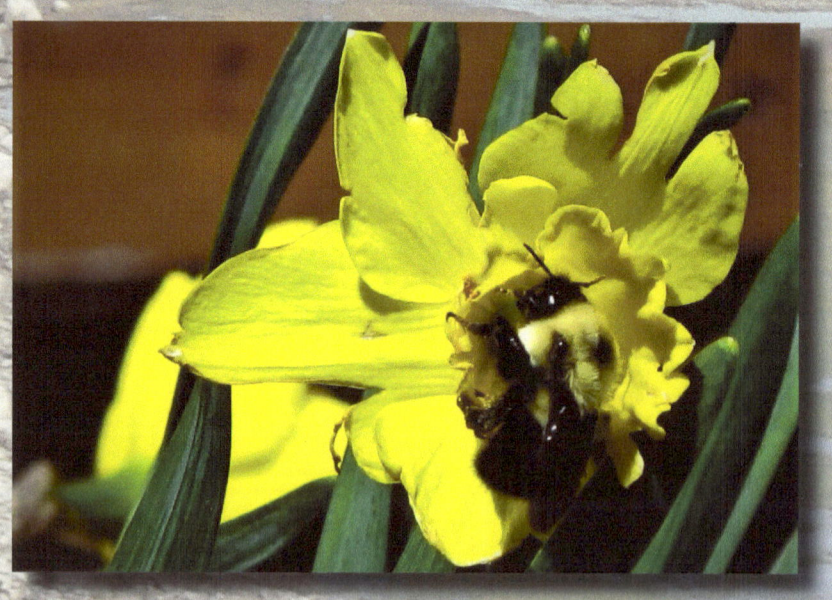

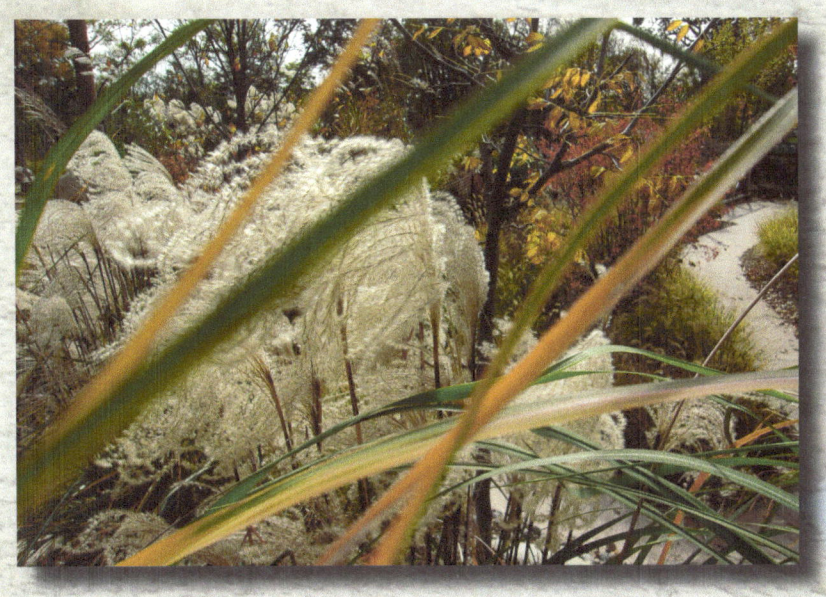

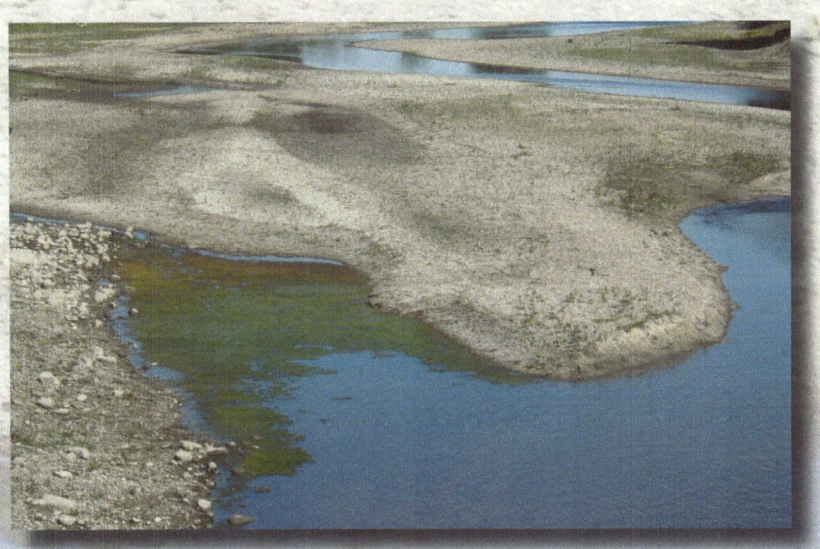

"Behold, I will do something new, now it will spring forth; will you not be aware of it? I will even make a roadway in the wilderness, rivers in the desert"
(Isaiah 43:19, NASB).

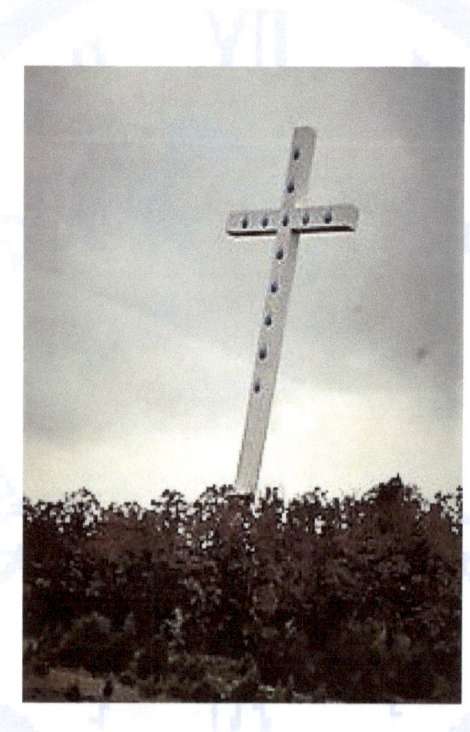

The perfect teaching and preaching of Jesus led Him on the perfect path. His perfect path led Him right to the cross (Philippians 2:5-11).

Jesus' Gospel message did not stop with His culture and time period. It continues today. Believers "talk the talk" and "walk the walk" of Jesus. They tell about the love of Jesus, and show His love.

Lift your eyes upward. Pray. Abide in the love of Jesus (John 15:9-10). Pray for opportunities to share His love.

It is never too late to begin again. While there is a beating heart, there is time for newness of that heart through the transforming power of Christ.

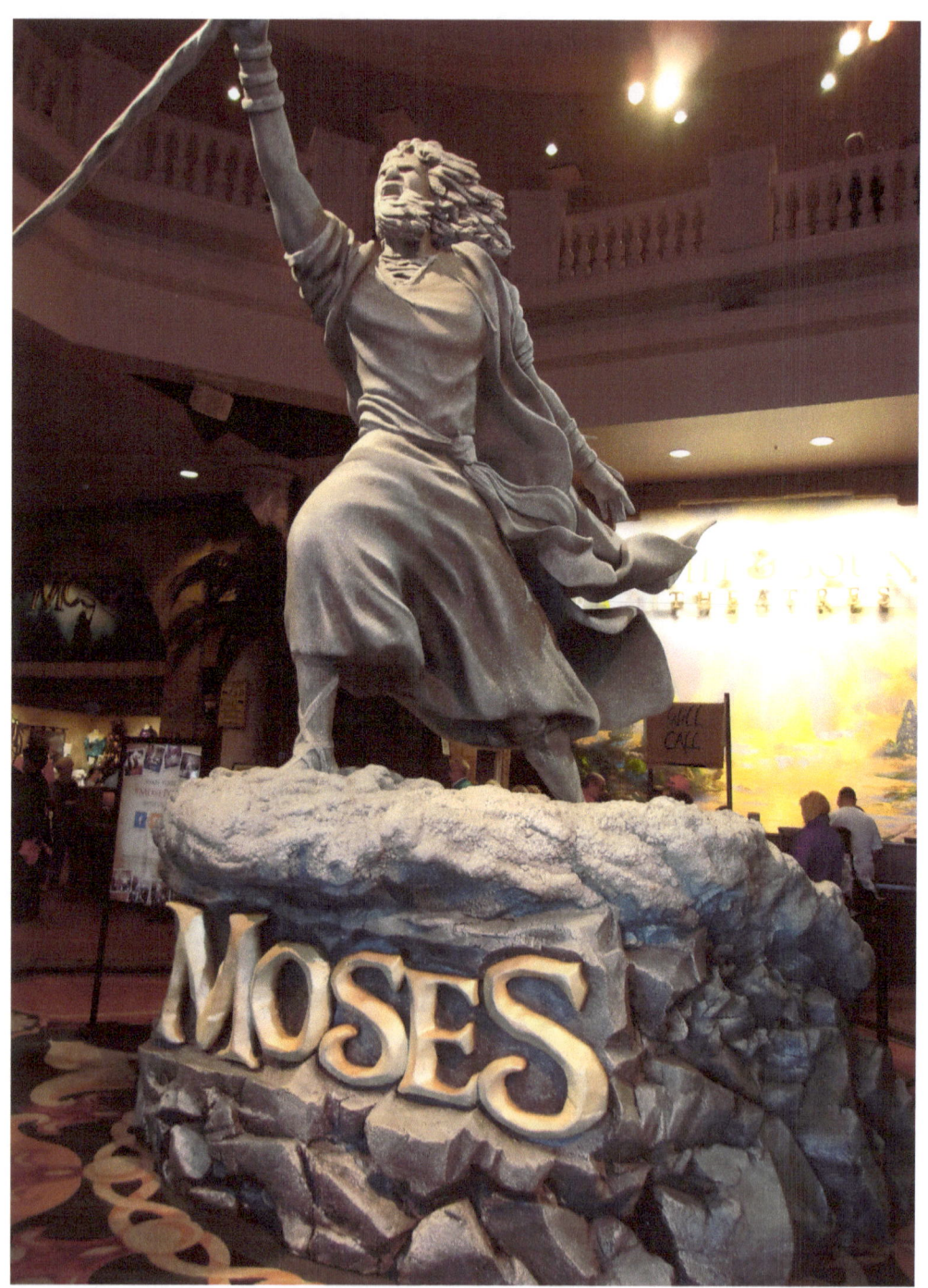

A Time ...

To listen. The month of *April* turns one's thoughts to outdoor spring activities, including baseball and other sporting events. Imagine sitting in front of a wide screen and viewing a prominent baseball game with all the wonderful sounds heard at live games. The fans cheer (or boo); the announcer speaks the names of the hitter, pitcher, or catcher; and loud music covers the entire baseball premises.

In another scenario, imagine yourself listening to your favorite music in a concert hall. The music meets your ears from all around. How sweet are the notes as they advance from one movement to the next. The sound crescendos from very quiet to an ever-increasing loudness. Suddenly, the music stops with an eerie silence that seems to last more than a moment.

The next best thing to **experiencing** live sound is listening to surround sound: a "system of sound recording and reproduction that uses three or more independent recording channels and loudspeakers in order to give the impression that the listener is surrounded by the sound sources."[1]

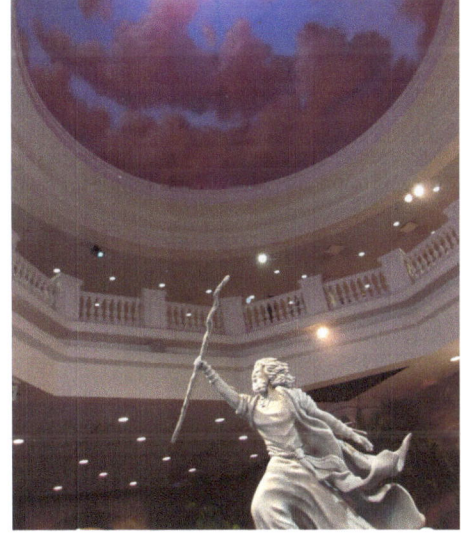

Use your imaginative ears now to hear surround sounds in the Bible—**big sounds**. "Then Moses stretched out his hand over the sea, and all that night the Lord drove the sea back with a strong east wind and turned it into dry land" (Exodus 14:21, NIV). Think also of the wall of water being held up on the right and on the left as the Israelites passed through the sea. Add to that the noise from Pharaoh's army, chariots, and horses. And bundle on that sound the voices of a huge crowd of frightened men, women, and children! From these deafening sounds there was no escape.

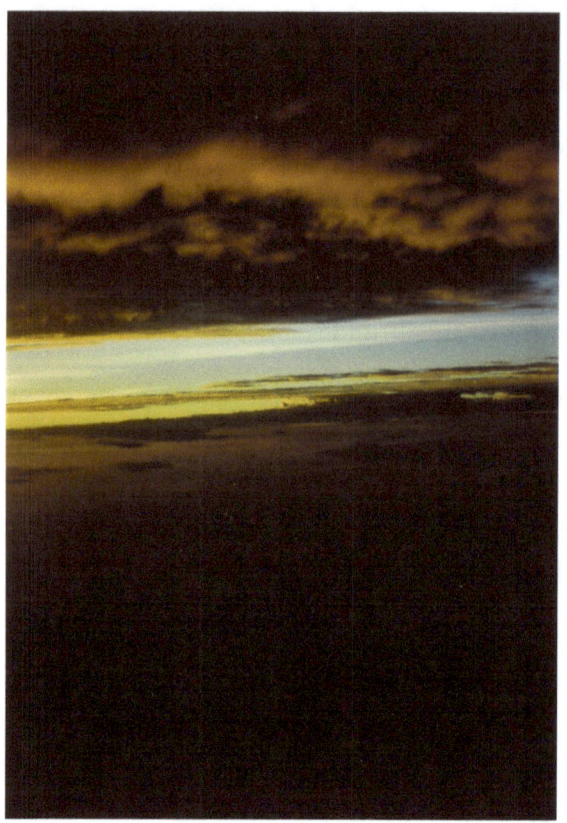

Now go to another scene in the Bible where "there were shepherds living out in the fields nearby, keeping watch over their flocks at night" (Luke 2:8, NIV). Do you hear the sheep bleating and the voices of shepherds?

Then, "an angel of the Lord appeared to them, and the glory of the Lord shone around them, and they were terrified" (Luke 2:9, NIV). "Suddenly a great company of the heavenly host appeared with the angel, praising God and saying, 'Glory to God in the highest, and on earth peace to men on whom His favor rests'" (Luke 2:13-14). What a sound that must have been!

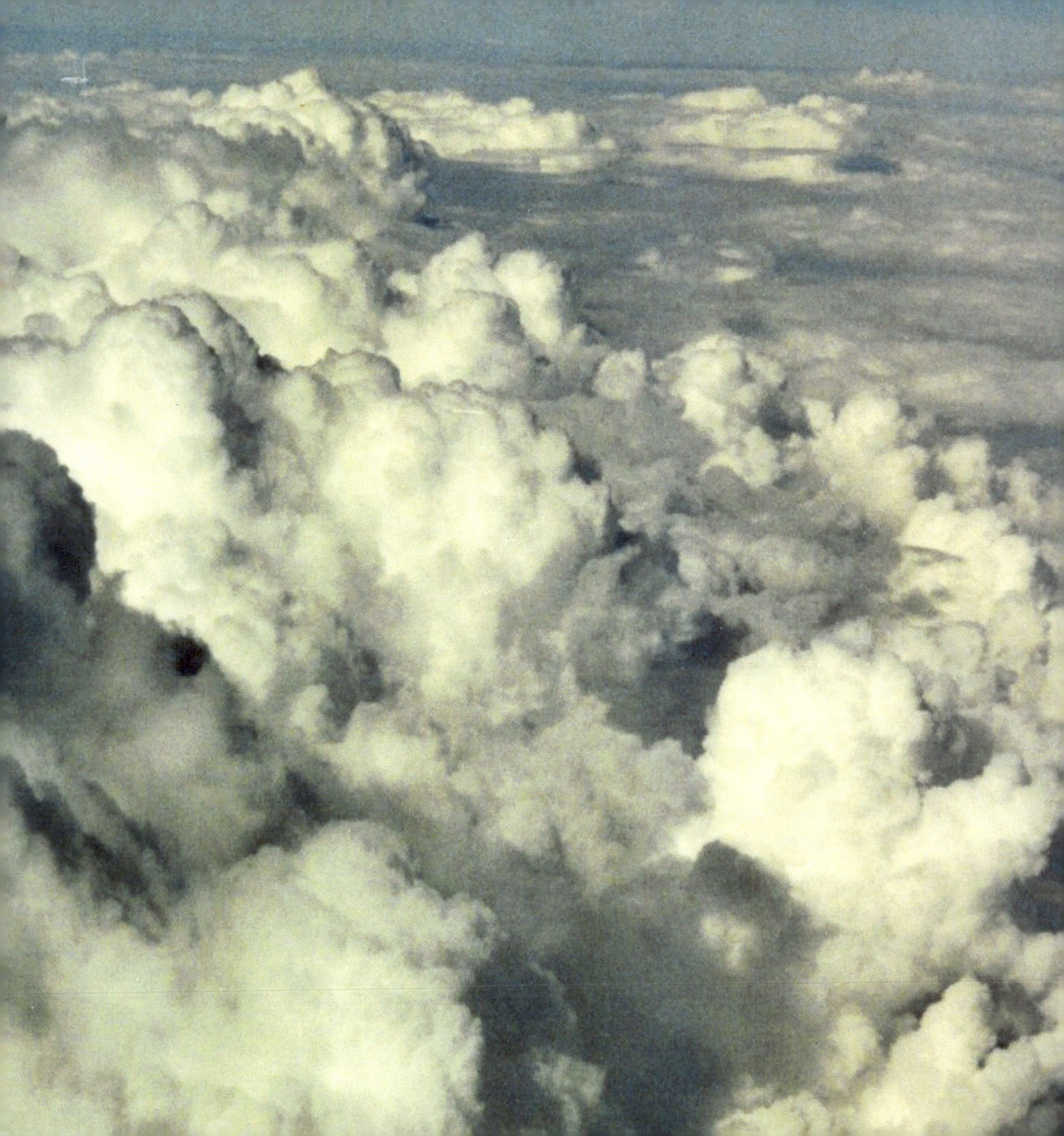

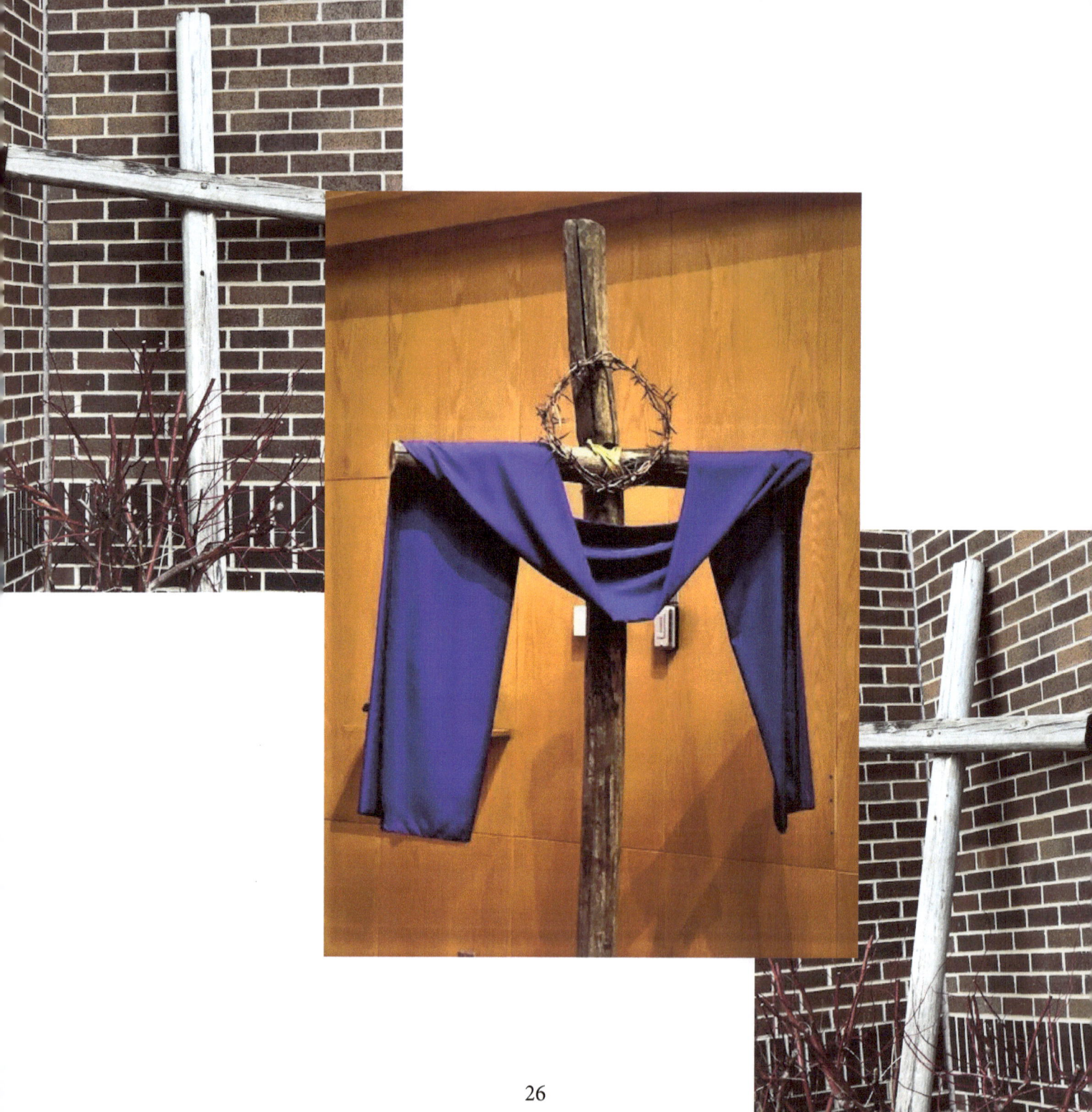

Move forward in biblical times to another crowd—a great crowd—who went out with palm branches to meet Jesus entering Jerusalem. The people shouted, "Hosanna! Blessed is He who comes in the name of the Lord! Blessed is the King of Israel" (John 12:13, NIV)!

If that sound was not loud enough, "hear" one more sound. In Matthew 27:20-26, Pilot asked the crowd what they wanted him to do with Jesus. They all answered, "Crucify him!" When Pilot asked why and what crime had he committed, "they shouted all the louder, 'Crucify him'" (Matthew 27:23)!

How does one turn off sounds of angry voices calling for the crucifixion of Jesus? Live sound may be exceptional, but with a surround sound system, fortunately, the noise can be quieted or discontinued.

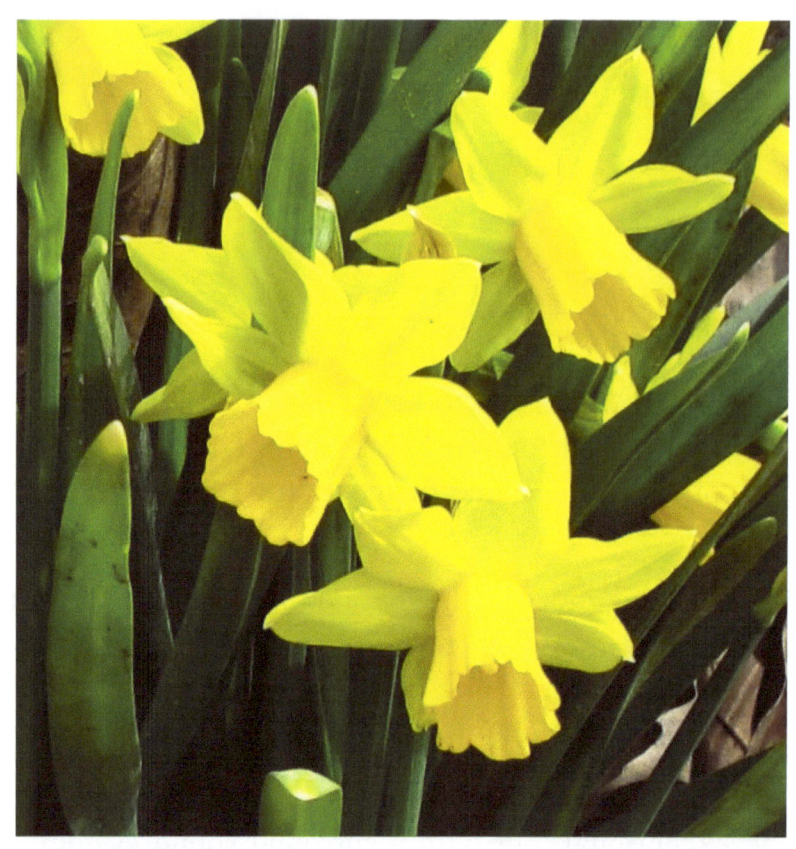

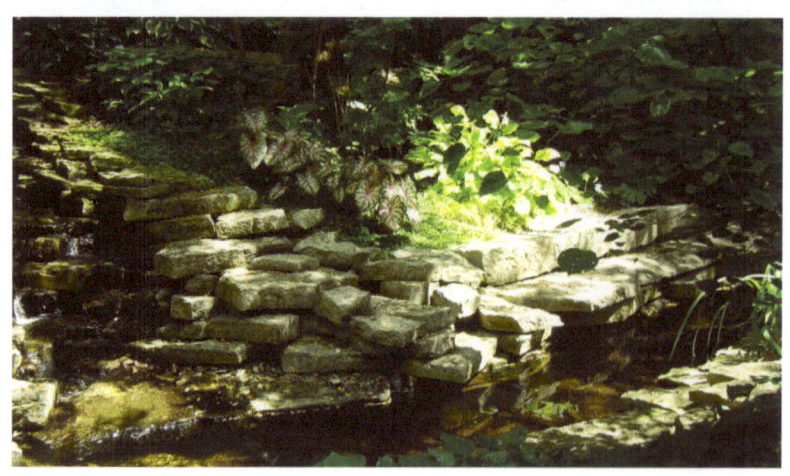

Thank Jesus for allowing Himself to be surrounded by the tune of death in order to save us. Without His death and resurrection, we sinners have no hope of life after death. Jesus has given us the gift of salvation. Bask in His love, and anticipate life with Him forever.

Listen—do you hear the sound of praises and thanksgiving from angels when the name of Jesus is mentioned?

Happy Easter!

He is risen indeed! Alleluia!

1 www.dictionary.com/browse/surround-sound.

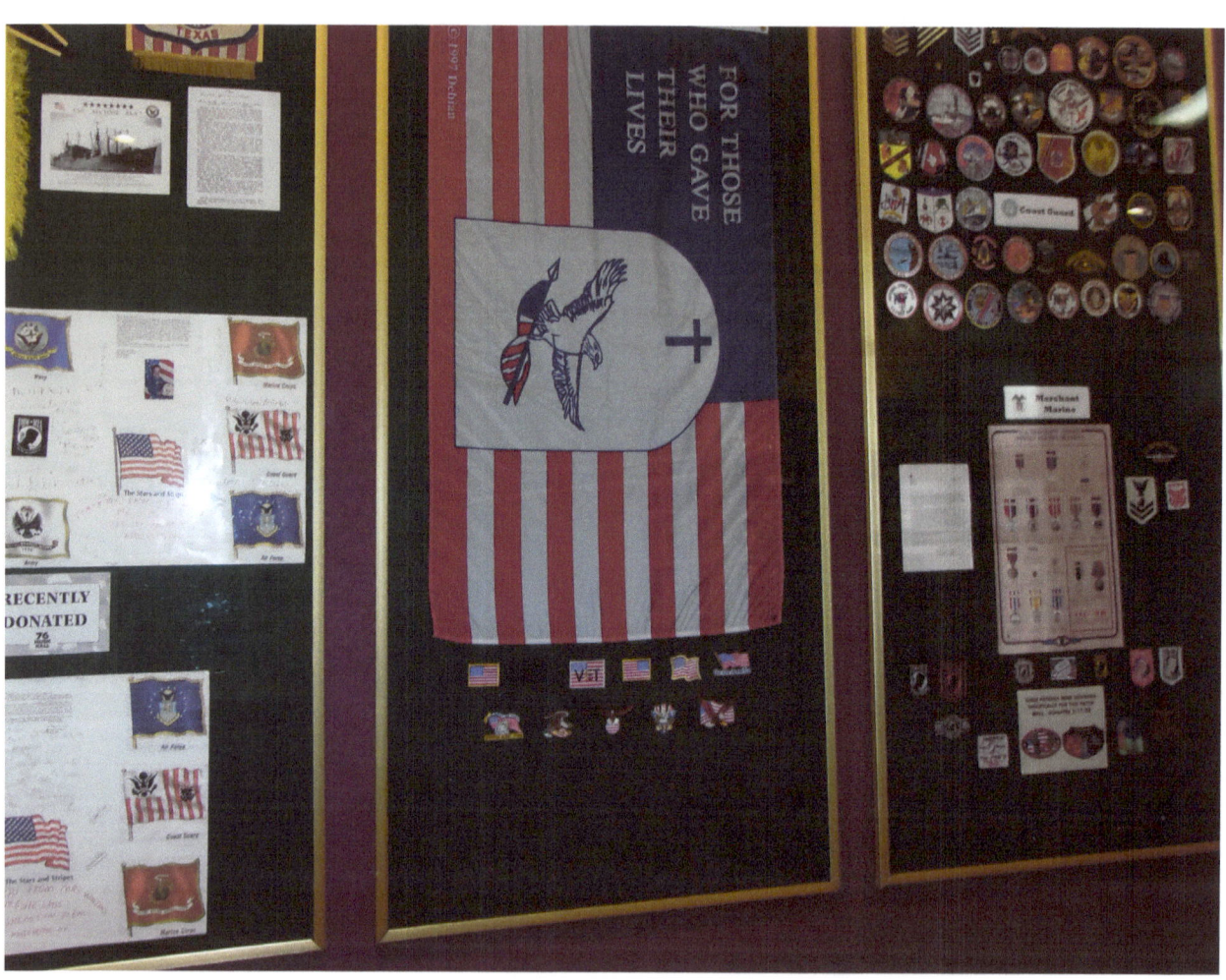

A Time ...

To remember. The month of *May* brings to mind a number of occurrences in America: National Day of Prayer,[1] Mother's Day,[2] and Memorial Day.[3] Remembering family, friends, and others who have died, helps one focus on those still alive.

Remembering helps bridge one generation to the next. World War II veterans are quickly disappearing. Their words reveal war tragedies through which they lived and scenes their eyes have not forgotten. Unless they discussed or wrote about their horrific war experiences, these events, and lives impacted by such events, will not be remembered one or two generations removed from that time period.

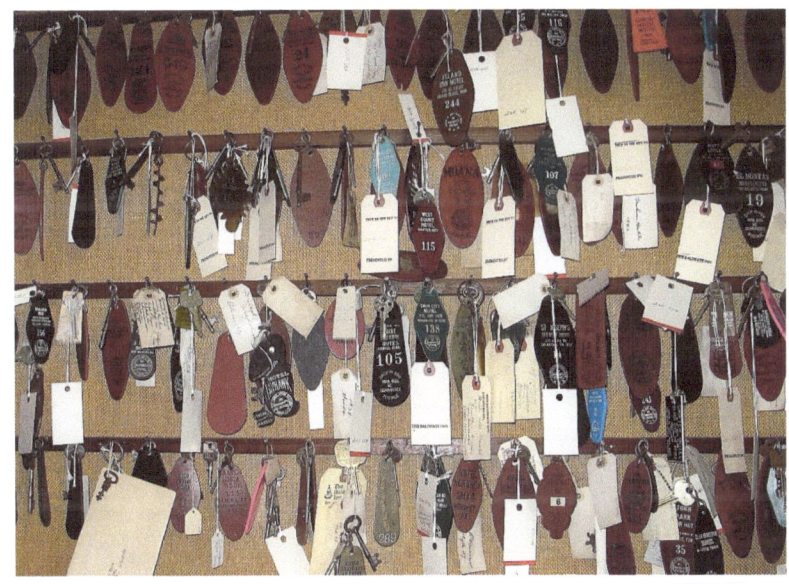

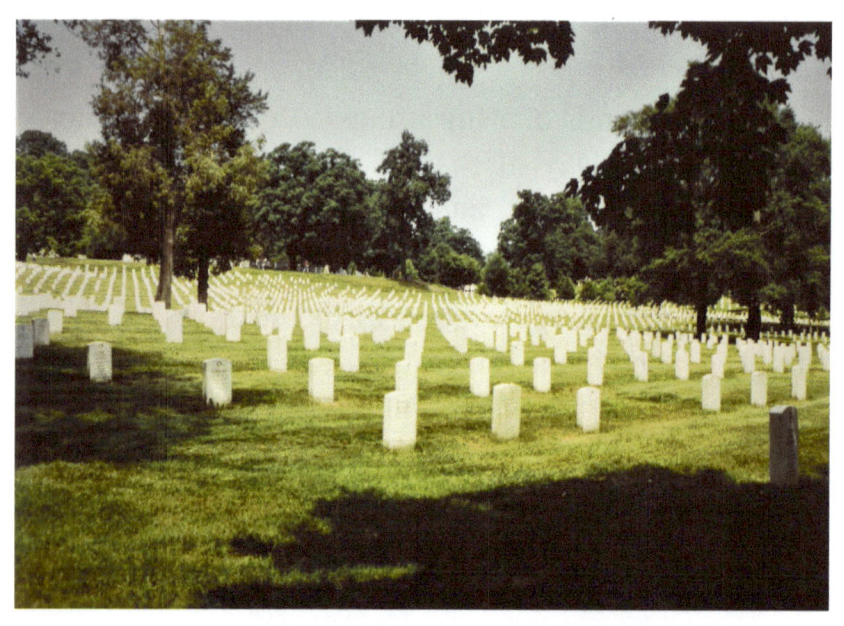

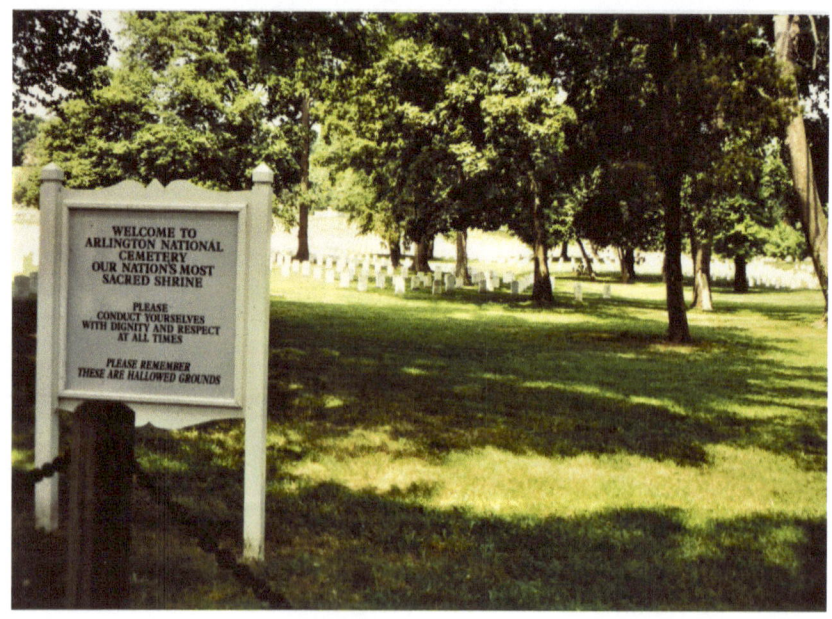

WELCOME TO
ARLINGTON NATIONAL
CEMETERY
OUR NATION'S MOST
SACRED SHRINE

PLEASE
CONDUCT YOURSELVES
WITH DIGNITY AND RESPECT
AT ALL TIMES

PLEASE REMEMBER
THESE ARE HALLOWED GROUNDS

Mothers, fathers, and grandparents, represent links in the communication chain to their children and grandchildren. In addition to information, God's commands, too, are to be relayed from one generation to the next (Deuteronomy 4:3-10). Through Moses, God revealed His greatness. Other nations observing God's people wondered what nation has their God near whenever they pray. What nation has such righteous decrees and laws. Moses cautioned the Israelites to remember:

"Only be careful, and watch yourselves closely so that you do not forget the things which your eyes have seen or let them slip from your heart as long as you live. Teach them to your children and to their children after them" (Deuteronomy 4:9, NIV).

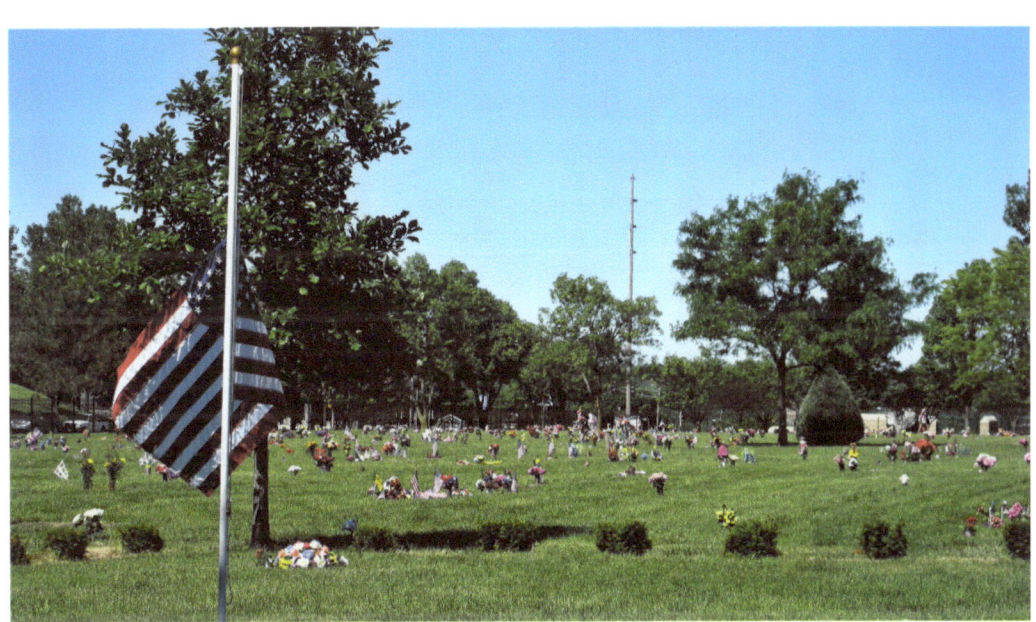

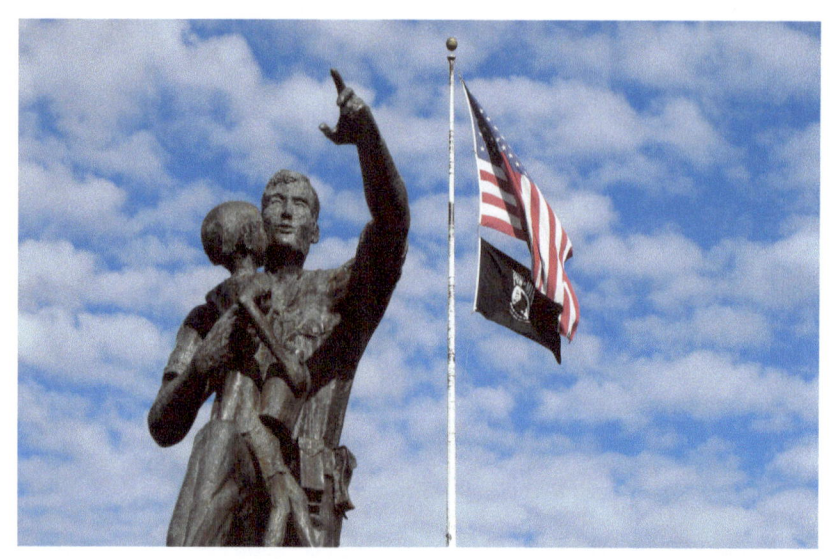

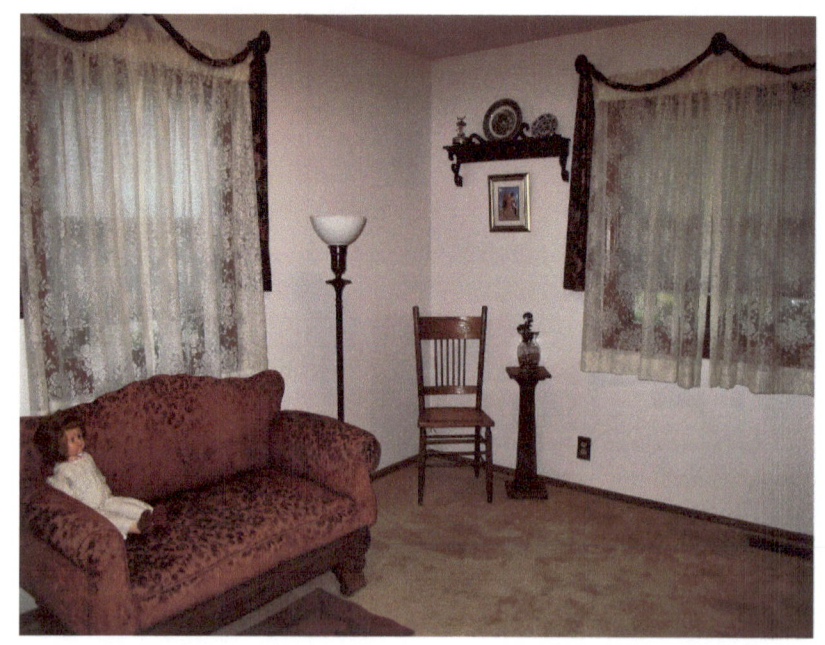

Along the lines of teaching, Jesus was a master teacher. At the age of 12, He sat in the temple among teachers, both listening to them and asking them questions (Luke 2:41-47). Jesus taught His disciples in words given to Him by His Father in heaven (John 17:8). He taught a multitude of people during the feeding of 5,000+ people with only five loaves of bread and two fish (Mark 6:33-38).

Teaching and remembering reinforce that spiritual chain between the past and the future (Psalm 78:1-8, NIV). If children do not know their roots, how will they know the amazing Christian foundations of America? How will they understand the works of God and His mighty power? If not taught the history of God's work in our nation, how will they remember and teach their children about these works?

Remembering that we exist for God's glory keeps us on the right path with our Creator. God created mankind as the pinnacle of this awesome world. Through prayer, a closer relationship develops with God. "Then you will call upon Me and come and pray to Me, and I will listen to you. You will seek Me and find Me when you seek Me with all your heart" (Jeremiah 29:12-13, NIV).

Take time to remember. Pause . . . and pray. Thank God for who He is and what He has done. Thank Him for mothers and those who have passed from this life. Remember especially those who have given their lives in love for America. Because of their sacrifice, we enjoy freedom. Remember...remember.

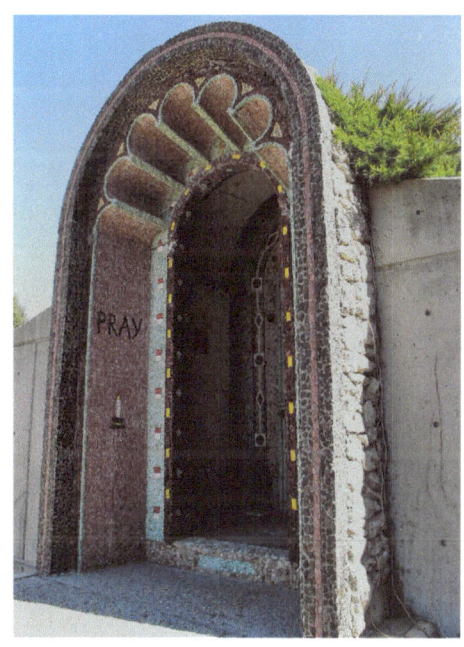

1 www.nationaldayofprayer.org.

2 www.timeanddate.com/holidays/us/mothers-day.

3 www.timeanddate.com/holidays/us/memorial-day.

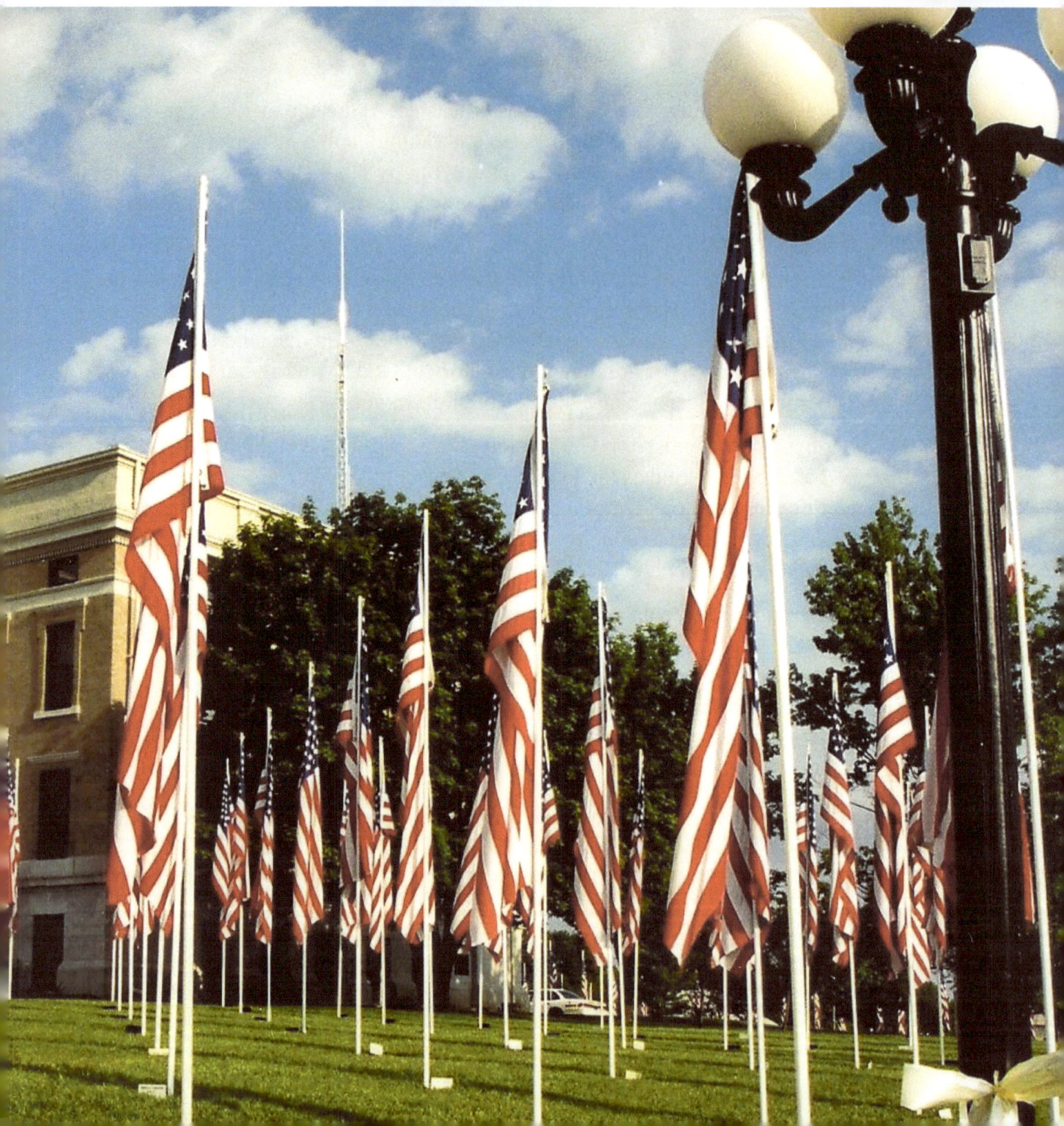

A Time ...

To ponder freedom, a flag and a father. The symbol of American freedom waves in the breeze as a striking flag arrayed in red, white, and blue. The first flag displayed thirteen stars and became the Official United States Flag on *June* 14, 1777. The governmental body known as the Continental Congress recognized by resolution an official flag for the new nation. This Continental Congress passed the first Flag Act: "Resolved, that the flag of the United States be thirteen stripes, alternate red and white; that the union be thirteen stars, white in a blue field, representing a new constellation." On August 3, 1949 President Harry S. Truman officially declared June 14 as Flag Day.[1]

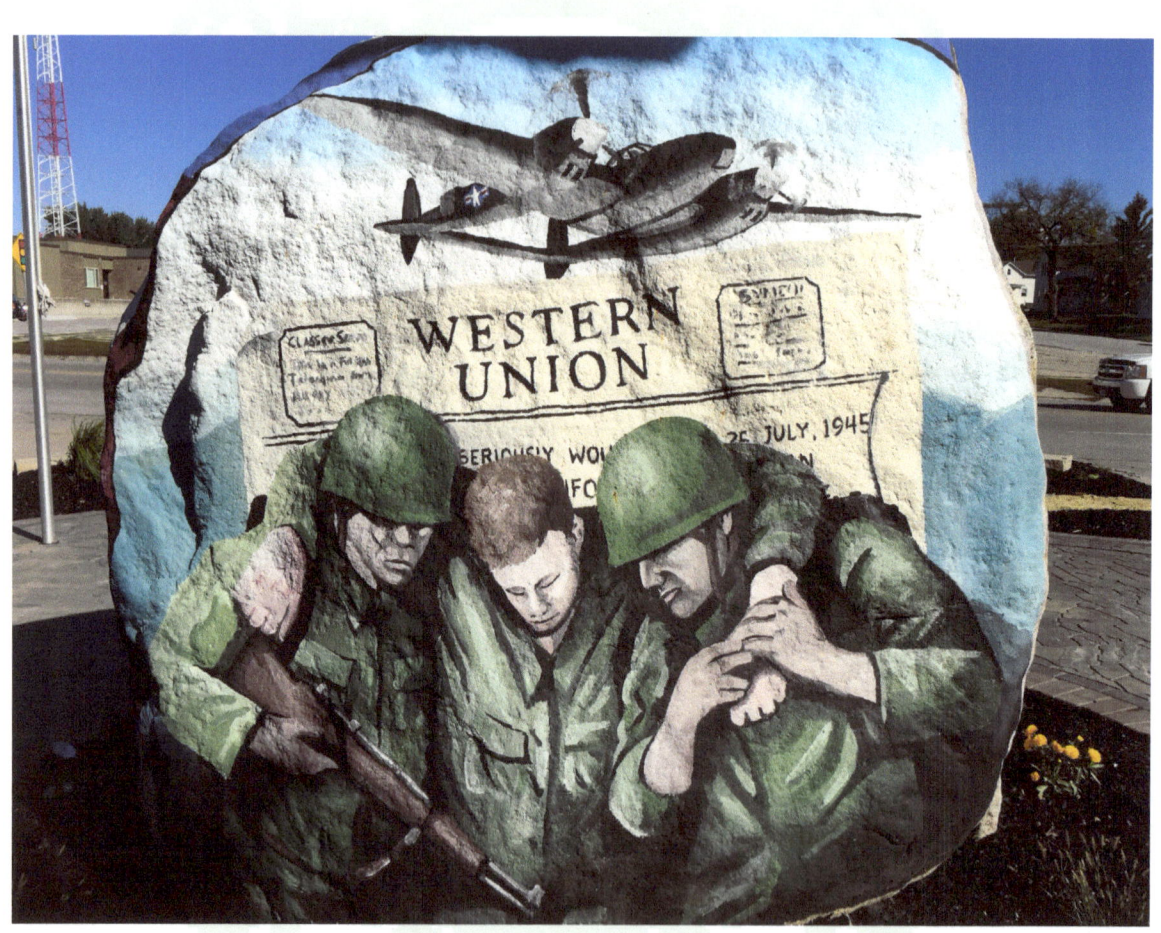

This red, white, and blue flag wraps within itself deep-seated emotions of pride, devotion, love, and honor. Oh, America! How we love you. What other country offers such freedoms! May freedom always be considered precious and costly in light of the many dear lives sacrificed for this freedom.

In this vein of the flag for freedom, consider the banner of love spread over us by Jesus Christ our Savior. Because He carried the burden of our sins to the cross, we have freedom from sin. Because Jesus rose from the dead, we have forgiveness of sins, and an inheritance with the heavenly Father lasting for eternity (Hebrews 12:2; 1 Corinthians 15:50-57; Colossians 2:13-15, Romans 5:8-11).

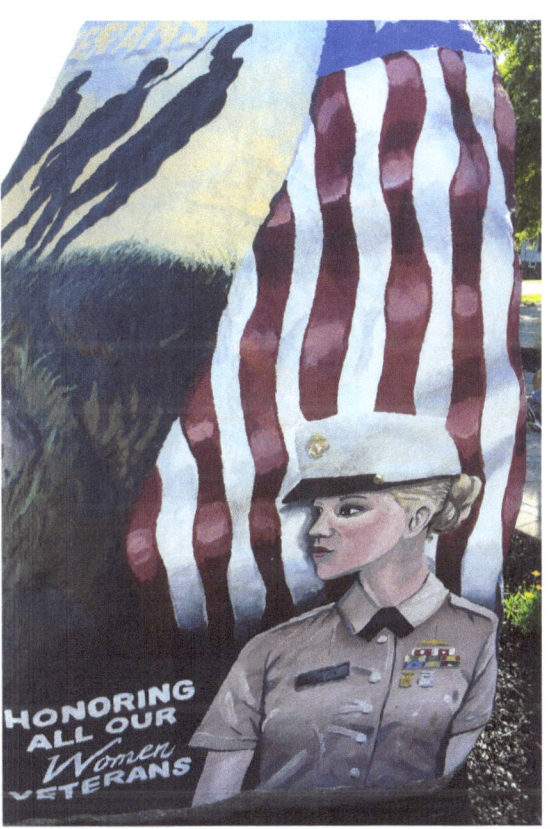

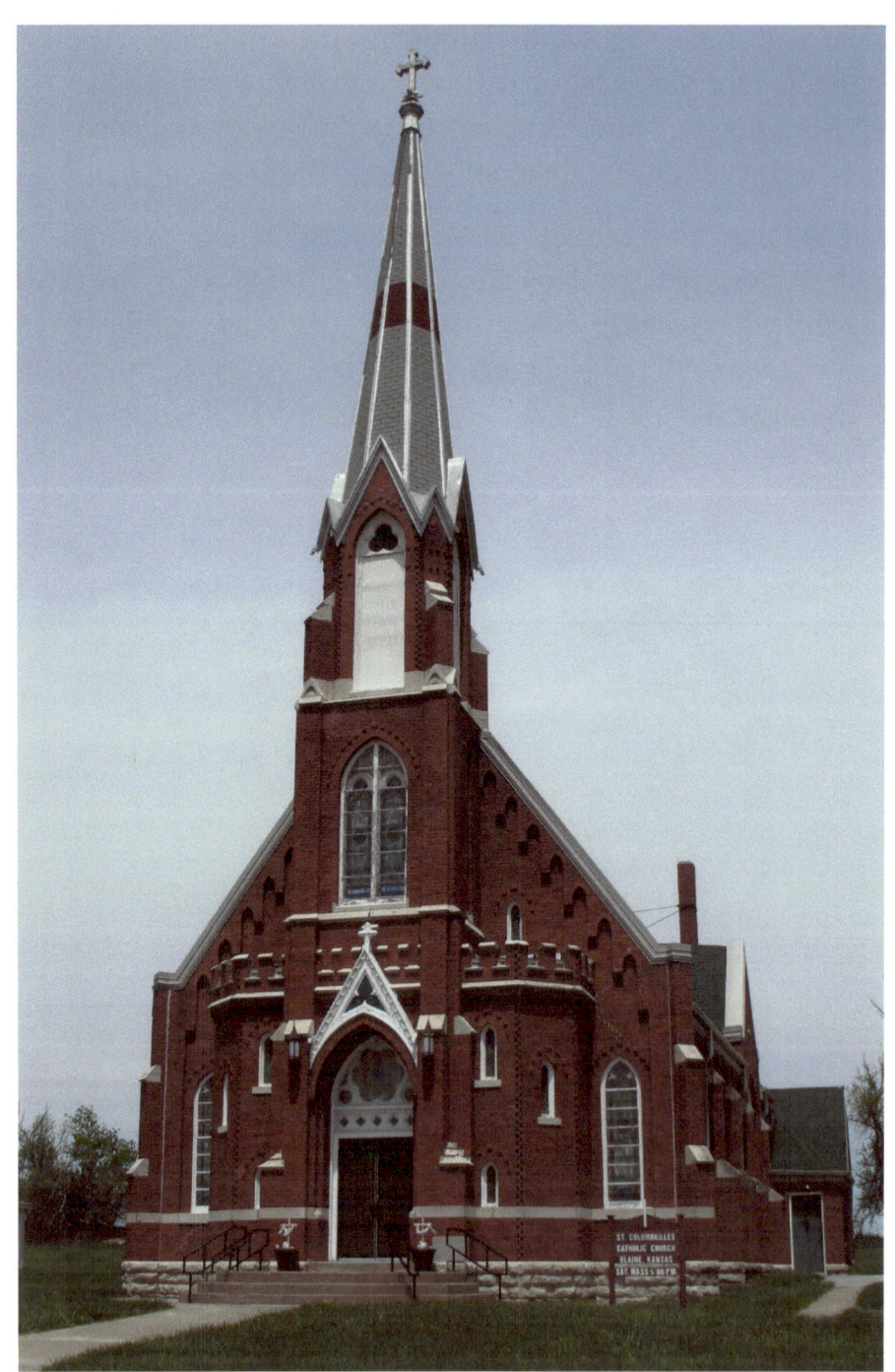

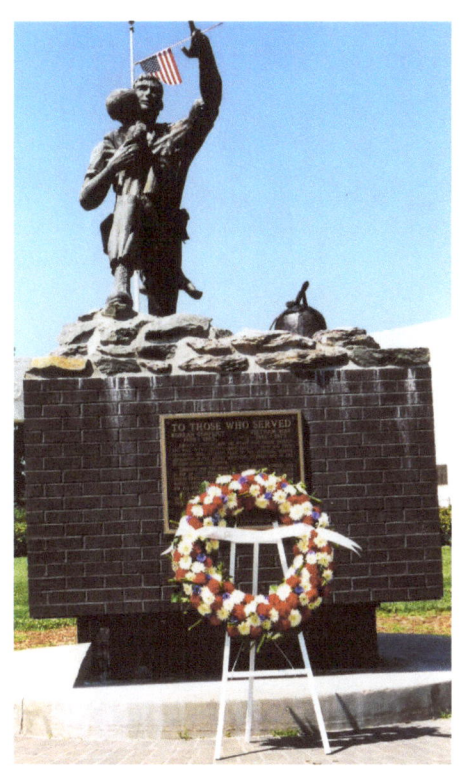

And speaking of fathers, "Father's Day in the United States is on the third Sunday of June. It celebrates the contributions fathers and father figures make for their children's lives. Its origins may lie in a memorial service held for a large group of men, many of them fathers, who were killed in a mining accident in Monongah, West Virginia in 1907."[2] The first Father's Day was celebrated in June 1910, but was officially recognized as a holiday in 1972 by President Nixon.[3]

The World Book Encyclopedia describes the word father as a "title of honor bestowed upon those of an earlier day who distinguished themselves as creators in some form of human endeavor, or who were associated in an exceptional way with important historic events. It is a title decreed by custom only."[4] Our Father in heaven is a Creator beyond compare. Who but He could create the earth, heavens, and entire solar system by a word!

When pondering freedom, the flag, and a father, think about Thanksgiving in June. Thankfulness for a country that still recognizes freedom: Congress shall make no law respecting an establishment of religion, or prohibiting the free exercise thereof; or abridging the freedom of speech, or of the press; or the right of the people peaceably to assemble, and to petition the Government for a redress of grievances.[5] Thankfulness for the banner of love Jesus wore on His way to the cross to win an eternal home in heaven for all who believe in Him. And also thankfulness for a heavenly Father beyond compare who so loved the world that He gave His only begotten Son, that whoever believes in Him should not perish but have everlasting life (John 3:16). Ponder . . . and again, ponder.

1 http://www.pbs.org/a-capitol-fourth/history/old-glory.

2 timeanddate.com/holidays/us/fathers-day.

3 Ibid.

4 The World Book Encyclopedia, Vol. 6 F, © 1934 by W.F. Quarrie & Company (Chicago, IL), pp.2379.

5 http://www.usconstitution.net/const.html.

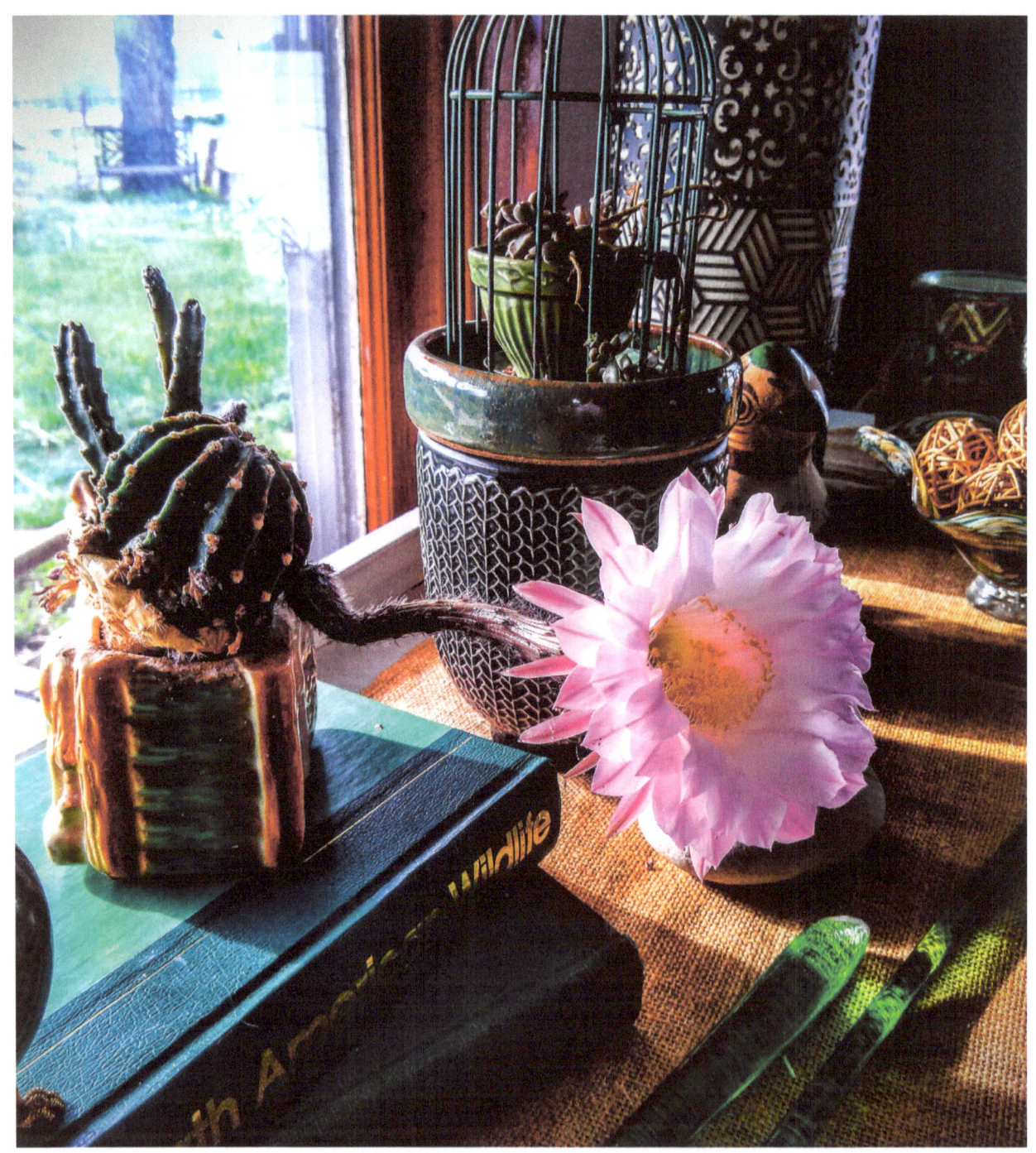

A Time ...

To wait, and a time to bloom. Many flowering plants are in full bloom for the month of *July*. During this time, blossoms which have come to the end of their blooming are pinched off and new blossoms replace those gone away. Some plants require a longer wait period before bursting into the bloom cycle again.

What about you? Are you blossoming, or are you waiting? What is that special passion in your life? What do you truly enjoy? What has God hard-wired into your inner being to drive and motivate you? Is it dormant—tucked away? Is that passion beginning to emerge? Does it want to come out? What about time—is your time occupied with "things" you love to do, "things" you have to do, or both?

Decisions? Choices? Priorities? God?

How do you make decisions and choices? What thoughts occupy your mind? Are they constructive thoughts, welling up into a full bloom of what you will do here on earth to glorify a gracious and loving God?

All these questions! For a moment or two, wait.

Wait? There seems to be *no* waiting time today. Answers to questions, or searches for knowledge, are instantaneously available through electronic devices. Tasks today need to be completed before dawn or late into the night.

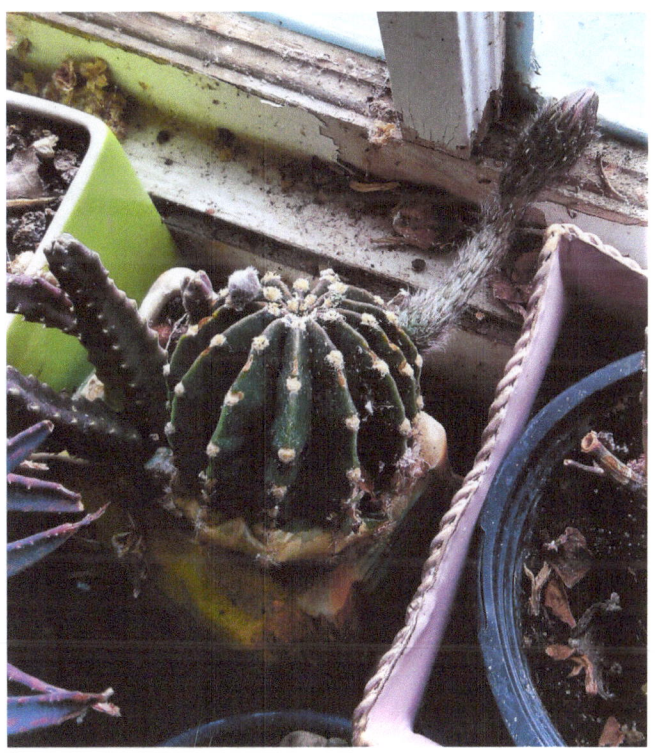

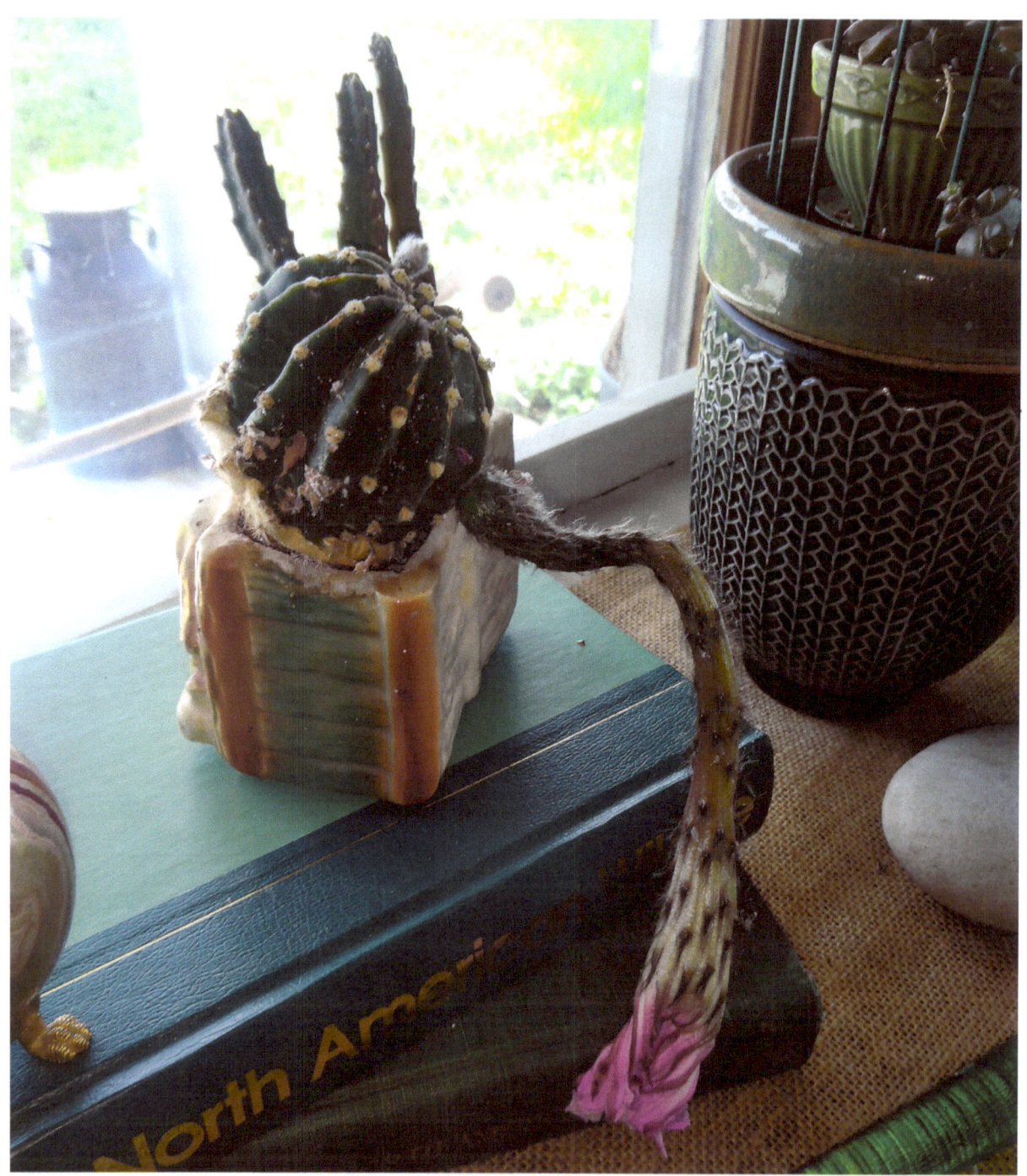

But pause and think about your passion. Pray about it. Ask God for direction and guidance. What does the Lord say about waiting?

"Be still before the Lord and wait patiently for Him; . . ."
(Psalm 37:7, NIV).

"Wait on the Lord; be of good courage, and He shall strengthen your heart; wait, I say, on the Lord" (Psalm 27:14, NKJV)!

"But those who wait on the Lord shall renew their strength; they shall mount up with wings like eagles, they shall run and not be weary, they shall walk and not faint"
(Isaiah 40:31, NKJV).

And what does He say about guidance? Below are a few Scripture passages regarding guidance.

"I will instruct you and teach you in the way you should go; I will guide you with My eye" (Psalm 32:8, NKJV).

"Your word is a lamp to my feet and a light to my path"
(Psalm 119:105, NASB).

"Your ears will hear a word behind you, 'This is the way, walk in it,' whenever you turn to the right or to the left" (Isaiah 30:21, NASB).

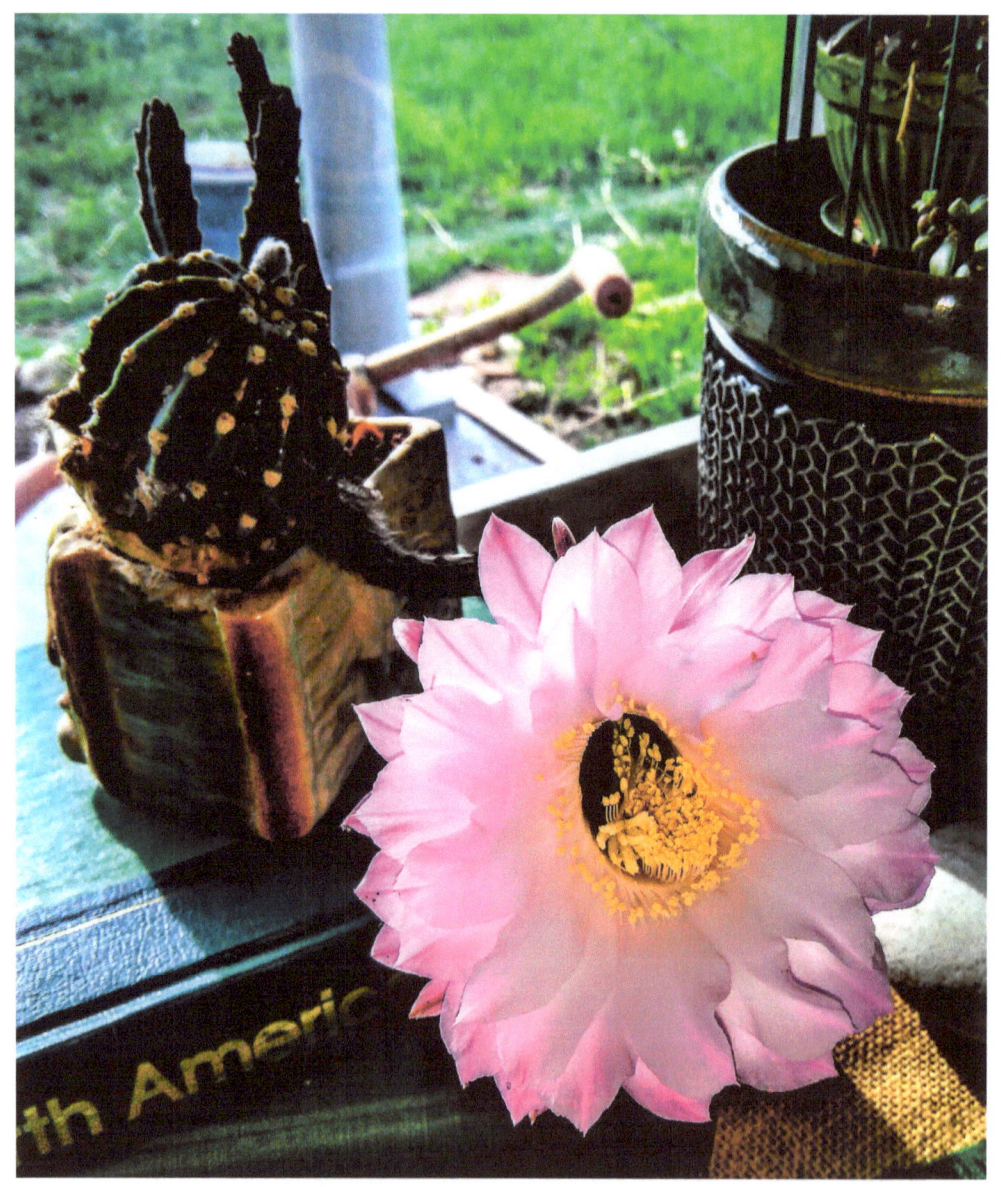

This following Scripture passage, in which Jesus is speaking, sounds delightful, and appears to take the load off one who is stressed to the maximum.

"Come to Me, all you who are weary and burdened, and I will give you rest. Take My yoke upon you and learn from Me, for I am gentle and humble in heart, and you will find rest for your souls. For My yoke is easy and My burden is light"
(Matthew 11:28-30, NIV).

But can these words from the Bible really be trusted and applied to life today?

If doubt creeps into your thinking, the Bible encourages to "trust in the Lord with all your heart, and lean not on your own understanding; in all your ways acknowledge Him, and He shall direct your paths" (Proverbs 3:5-6, NKJV).

The bloom is in the making. Just as a plant needs soil, water, light, and food to grow and blossom, so do you have needs. Follow the Light of the world (John 8:12), drink the water that Jesus gives (John 4:13-14), and feed upon God's Word (Joshua 1:8). Watch, wait, and pray for your special blooming season.

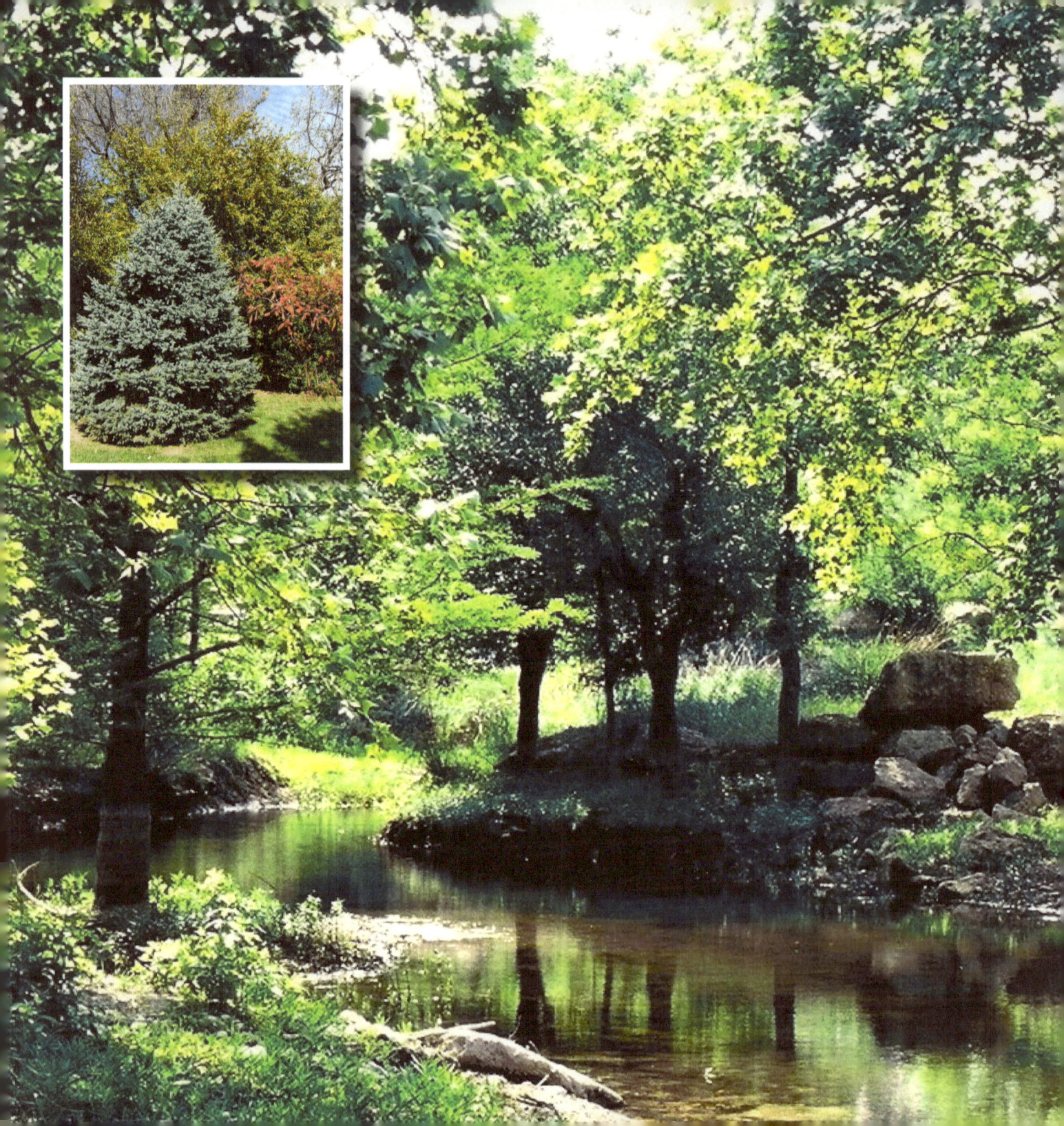

A Time ...

To rest. Summer is waning. Days are noticeably shorter in the month of *August.* Have you enjoyed the summer? Have you accomplished all you desired—trips, vacations, projects, visits with family and friends? Stop for a moment; don't go there.

Instead, inhale very deeply. Feel the air expand into your abdominal cavity. For just a moment, did you forget everything else as you concentrated on moving air into that particular part of your body? Cares and concerns seem to disappear as you focus on the act of breathing deeply. "Breathing from the abdomen, low back and sides while bringing in as much fresh air as possible must be learned or relearned.... Different breathing techniques open our body's breathing spaces. Some exercise can also work on our spirituality and inner peace to help us rejuvenate and live a more fulfilling life."[1]

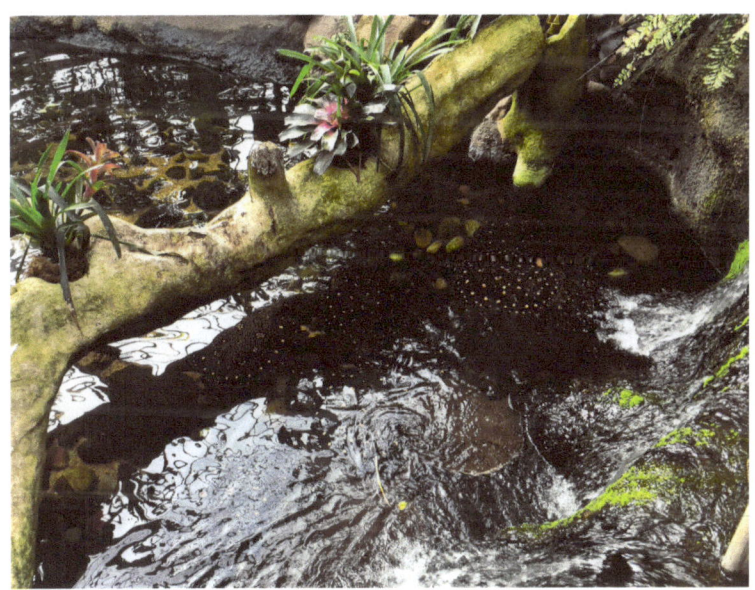

Now think of the Bible as an oasis for inner peace, a resting stop for each and every day. In other words, delay for just a short time today's wearisome journey. There are *many* "green" spaces or "watering" holes in the Bible from which to graze or drink deeply.

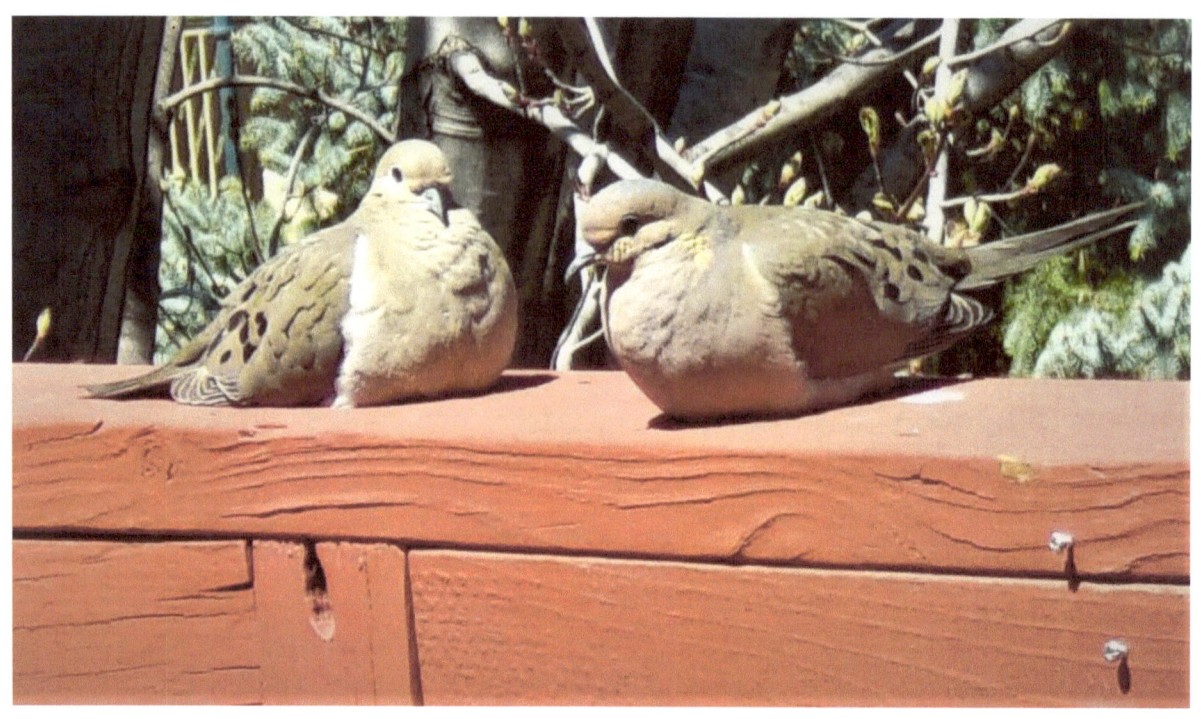

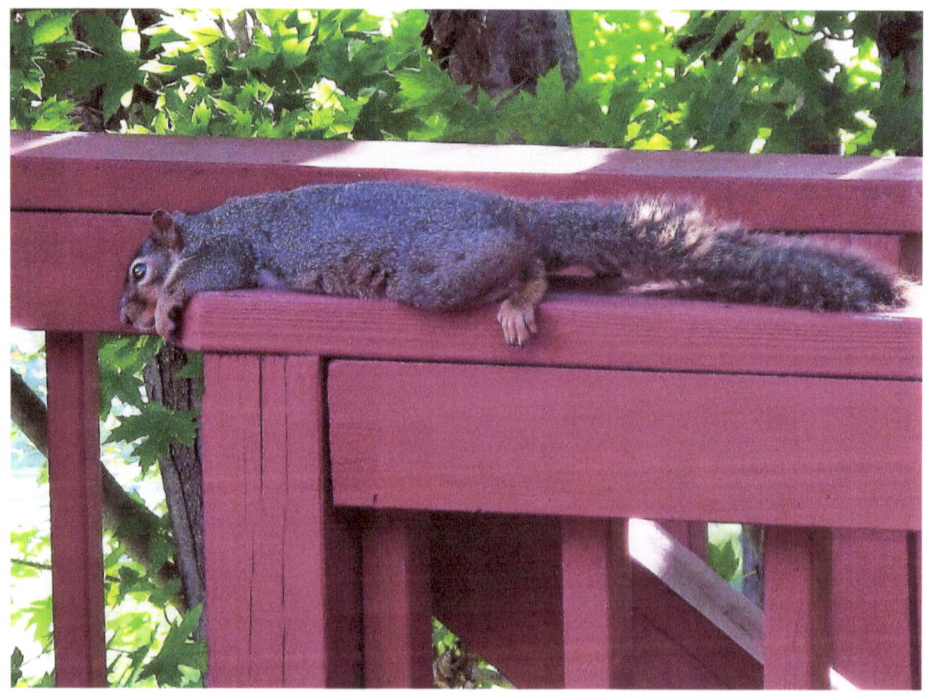

Two resting places include:

Psalm 62:1—My soul finds rest in God alone; my salvation comes from Him (NIV).

Matthew 11:28—Come to Me, all you who labor and are heavy laden, and I will give
you rest (NKJV).

Resting gives your body and mind a break in continuous movement. Yes, your heart continues to beat as your blood pulsates throughout your body. However, this movement slows. Time becomes your friend as you savor the moments to be used to be still and drink deeply from God's Word.

Take the time each day to find your green space, even if only for 15 minutes. Bask in Scripture and rest under words such as, "For He satisfies the longing soul, and fills the hungry soul with goodness" from Psalm 107:9 (NKJV). Rest and breathe deeply of God's grace.

1 www.breathing-exercises.com/Deeper_breathing.html.

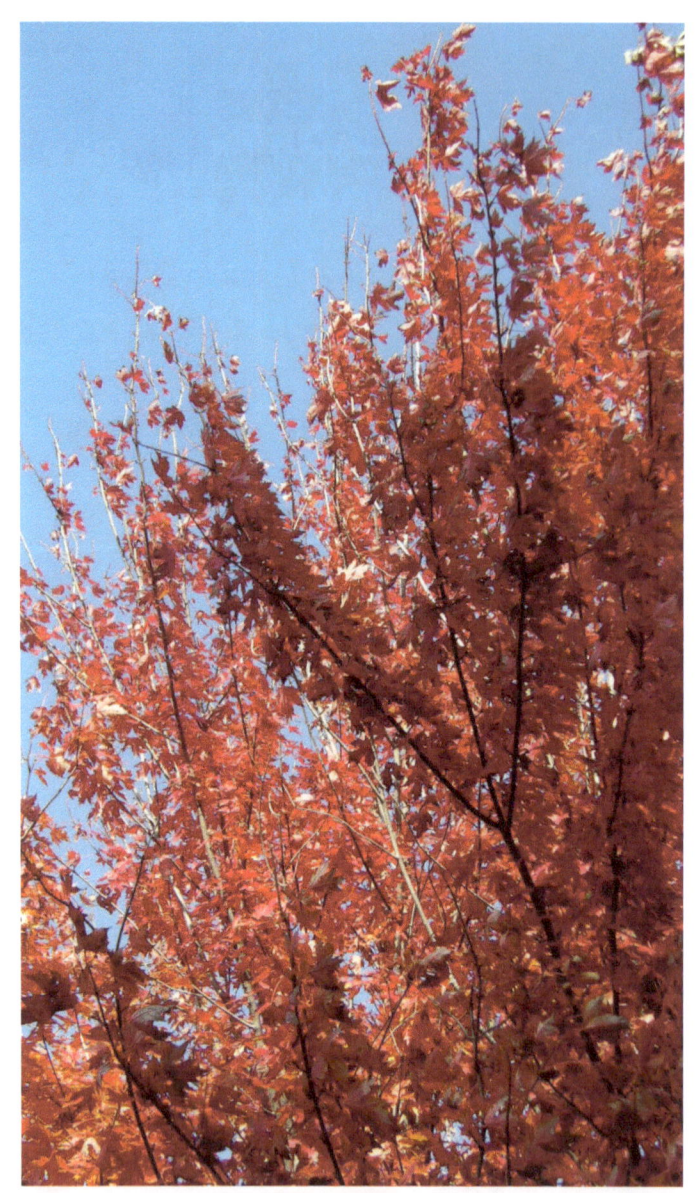
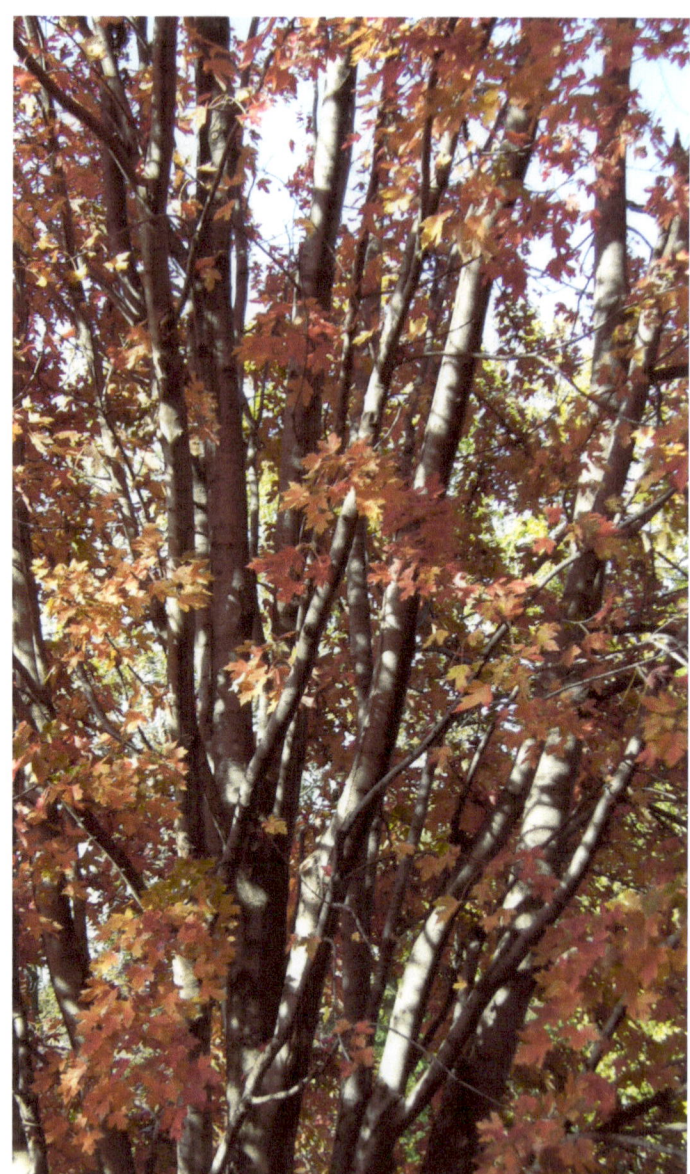
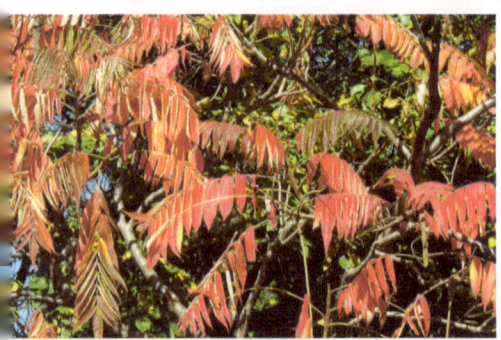
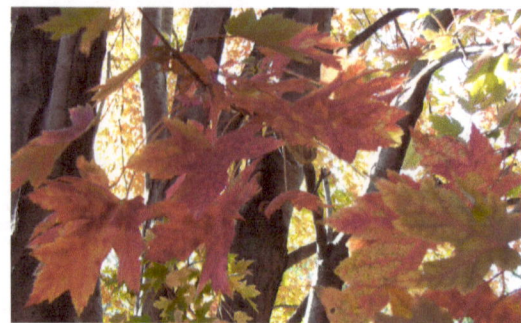
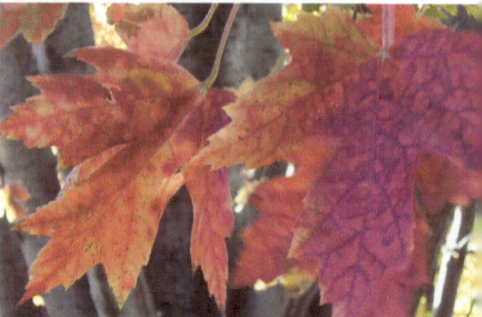

A Time ...

To change. **September** in various states of North America signals the beginning of autumn—a season between summer and winter. In Nebraska, leaves on trees change from green to vivid hues of red, orange, and yellow. This is a time to be outdoors among the trees. Breathe in that crisp fall air. Bask your eyes on the lovely creation God has made for our enjoyment and delight.

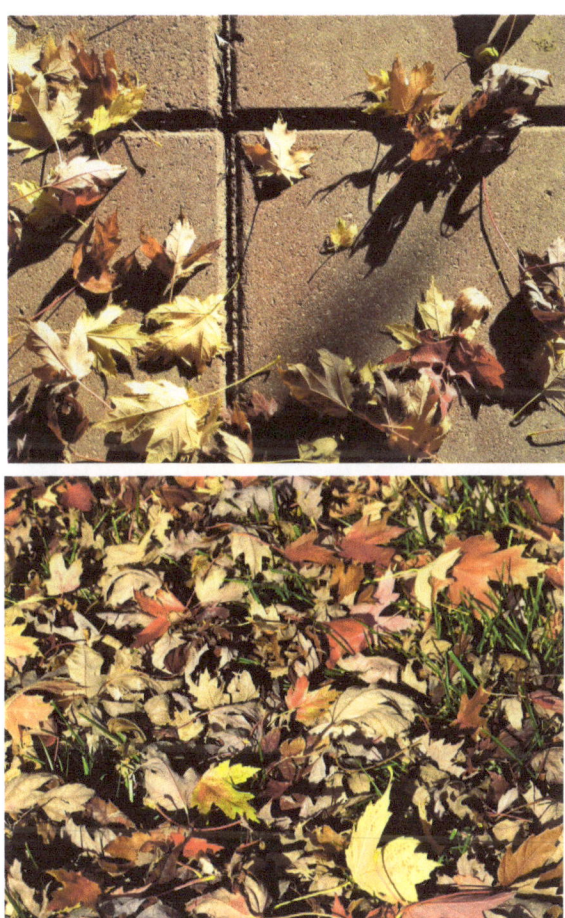

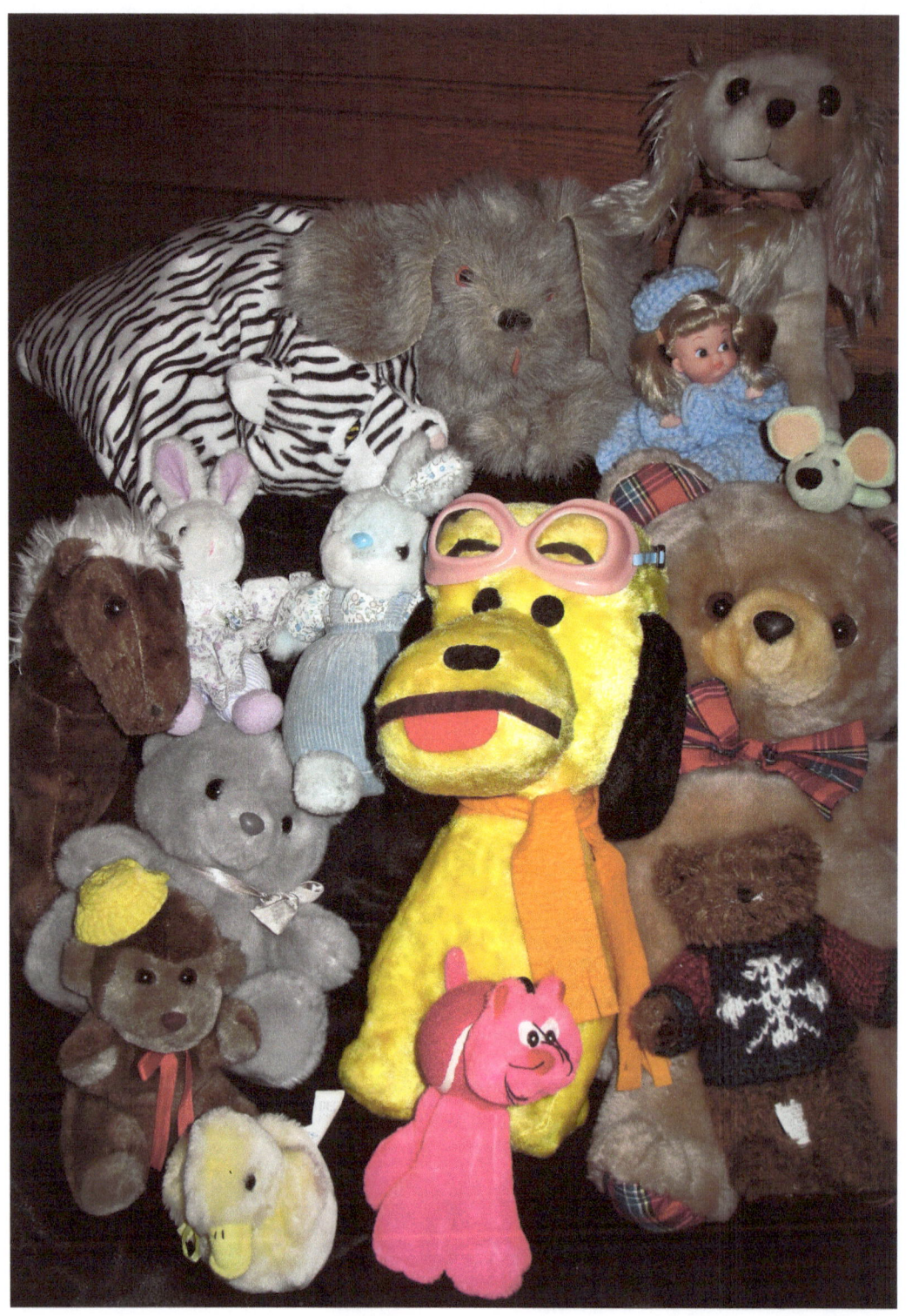

Humans make up the crowning portion of God's beautiful creation. Change continues each day in our human bodies. Various bodily seasons occur over time—that of an infant, to the season of a child, to an adult, and finally, to a senior citizen. Depending upon God's timetable for each individual's life, one may or may not experience these four passages of time.

The Bible speaks in several instances about change for our bodies. Paul writes to believers in Christ: "And we...are being transformed into His likeness with ever-increasing glory, which comes from the Lord, who is the Spirit" (2 Corinthians 3:18, NIV).

Paul also describes change to Corinthian believers in Christ as follows:

"Behold, I tell you a mystery; we will not all sleep, but we will all be changed, in a moment, in the twinkling of an eye, at the last trumpet; for the trumpet will sound, and the dead will be raised imperishable, and we will be changed. For this perishable must put on the imperishable, and this mortal must put on immortality. But when this perishable will have put on the imperishable, and this mortal will have put on immortality, then will come about the saying that is written, 'Death is swallowed up in victory. O death, where is your victory? O death, where is your sting'" (1 Corinthians 15:51-55, NASB)?

"Beloved, now we are children of God, and it has not appeared as yet what we will be. We know that when He appears, we will be like Him, because we will see Him just as He is" (1 John 3:2, NASB).

"Therefore we do not lose heart. Though outwardly we are wasting away, yet inwardly we are being renewed day by day. For our light and momentary troubles are achieving for us an eternal glory that far outweighs them all. So we fix our eyes not on what is seen, but on what is unseen. For what is seen is temporary, but what is unseen is eternal"
(2 Corinthians 4:16-18, NIV).

God created humans with a life-sustaining organ known as the heart. This heart is not inanimate. It gives life and vigor. The heart can be good—or not. It can be warm, or cold (after death). The heart was created with a "changeable" attribute. Ezekiel 36:26 refers to a new heart of flesh replacing the heart of stone. The Ancient One, the true God of the Bible, can change a heart of stone. Time, experiences, and troubles may soften a heart for the betterment of an individual and for the glory of God.

The heart is quite revealing of an individual's character as noted in Proverbs 23:7 (NKJV): "For as he thinks in his heart, so is he." In 1 Samuel 13:13-14, and 1 Samuel 16:1 and 13, King David is described as "a man after God's own heart."

A changed heart usually involves prayers. The prayers may be from that individual, or prayers from another. "Prayer doesn't merely change things, it will change us. As we pray, God reveals His will and ways to us, and then starts to align our hearts and minds with His. . . . The more time we spend with God, the more humble, unselfish, and like Jesus we will become."[1]

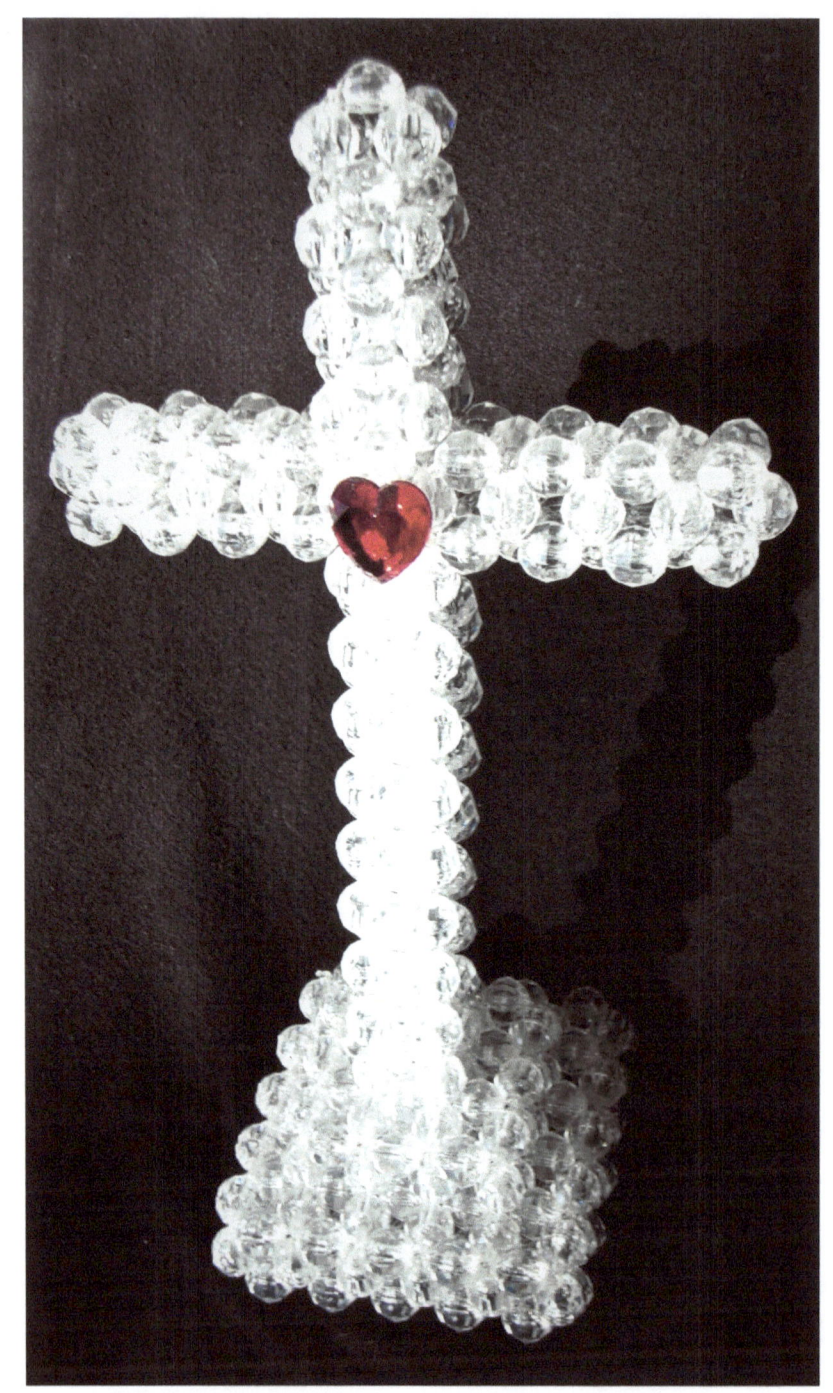

58

And as we focus on God, we will bask in the change of a new lifestyle—becoming that lovely creation God intended us to be. Amazingly, while we and all else on this earth continue to change, God does not.

1 The Battle Plan for Prayer © 2015 by Kendrick Brothers, LLC; B&H Publishing Group (Nashville, TN), p. 37.

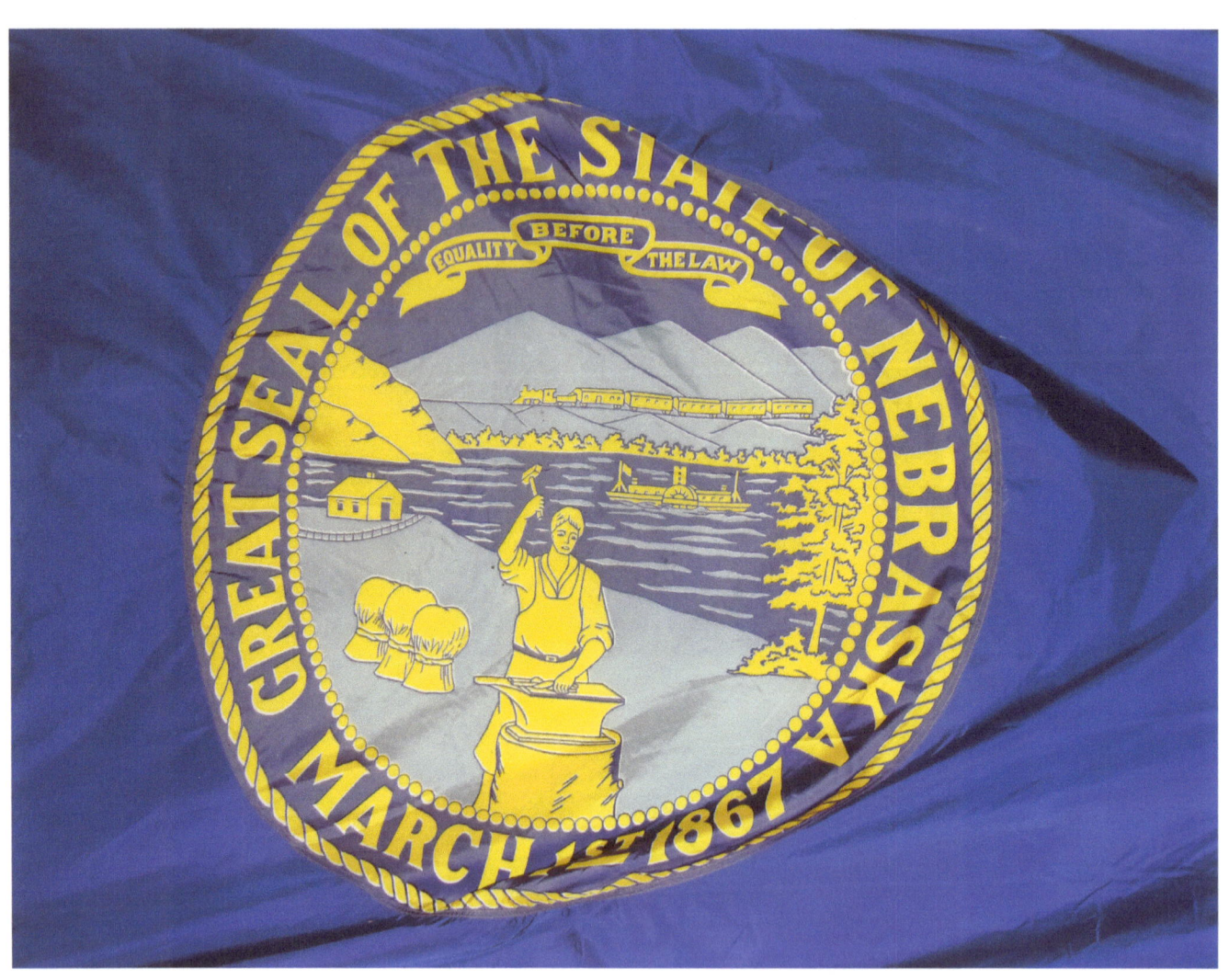

A Time ...

For truth. Columbus discovered America **October** 12, 1492. But was his discovery really the first? Historical proof is still debated.[1]

Nebraska was admitted to the union as the 37th state on March 1, 1867, two years after the end of the American Civil War.[2]

Truth seems to be elusive today. "Fact checkers" were important during news broadcasts in the 2016 presidential election process to discover who was telling the truth.

During the days of Jesus, truth was a common subject, too.

Jesus answered [Pilot], "You say rightly that I am a king. For this cause I was born, and for this cause I have come into the world, that I should bear witness to the truth. Everyone who is of the truth hears My voice" (John 18:37, NKJV).

Jesus mentions truth when praying to God the Father for His disciples, "Sanctify them by Your truth. Your word is truth" (John 17:17, NKJV).

And again, when Jesus answers a question from Thomas, "I am the way, the truth, and the life. No one comes to the Father except through Me" (John 14:6, NKJV).

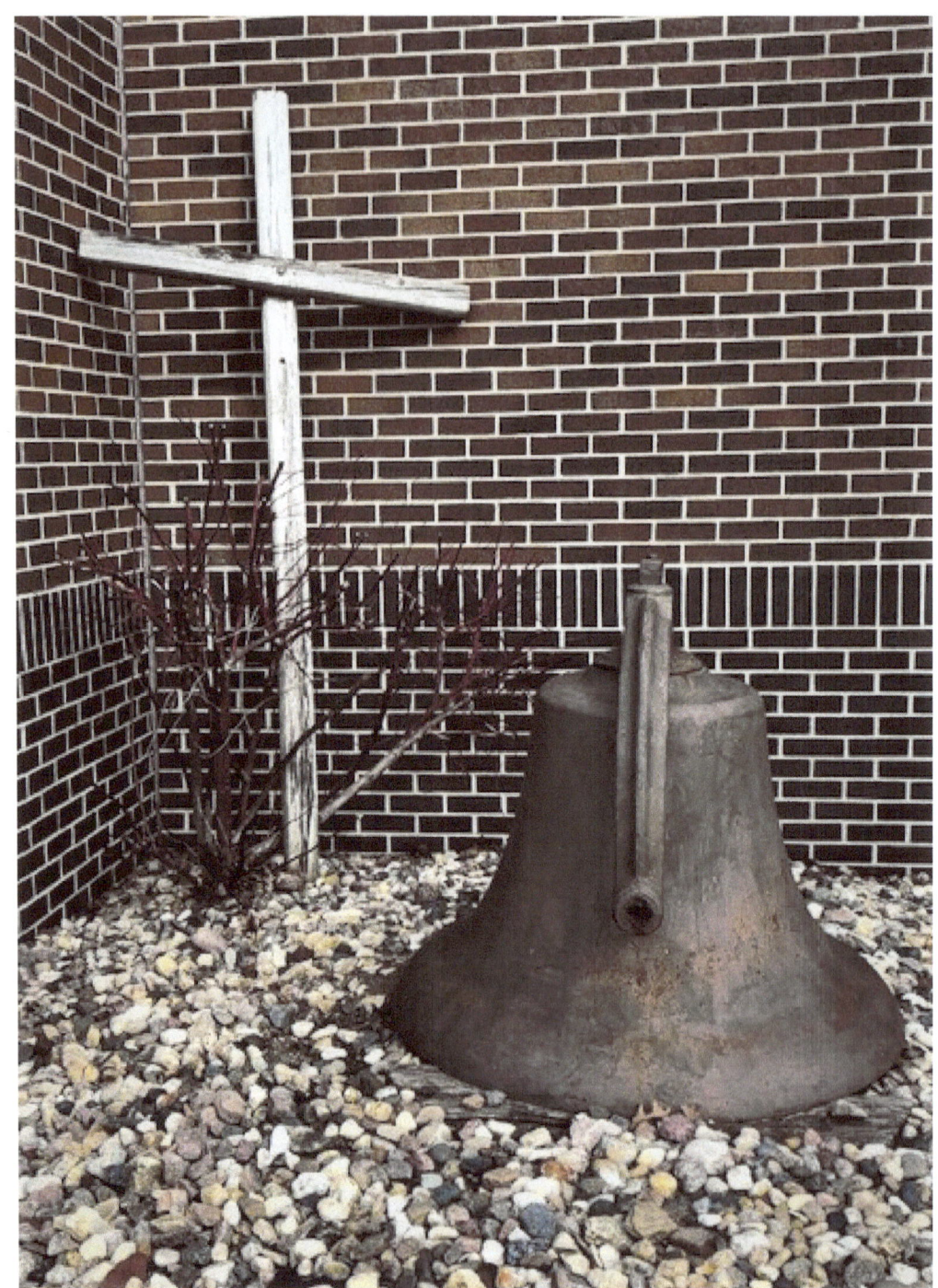

Songs, too, speak of truth. Words from a song entitled **Ancient Words** summarize the truth concept as follows: "Ancient words, ever true, changing me, changing you; we have come with open hearts, O let the ancient words impart."[3]

The truth is that Jesus desires all to be saved (1 Timothy 2:4-6). His desire will one day be fulfillment for all believers in Him (John 3:15-17).

Take action. Spread the love of a Savior who cares. Truth can mean the difference between eternal life or eternal death.

1 www.americanheritage.com/content/was-america-discovered-columbus.

2 www.history.com/topics/us-states/nebraska.

3 Ancient Words; Lynn DeShazo (2001).

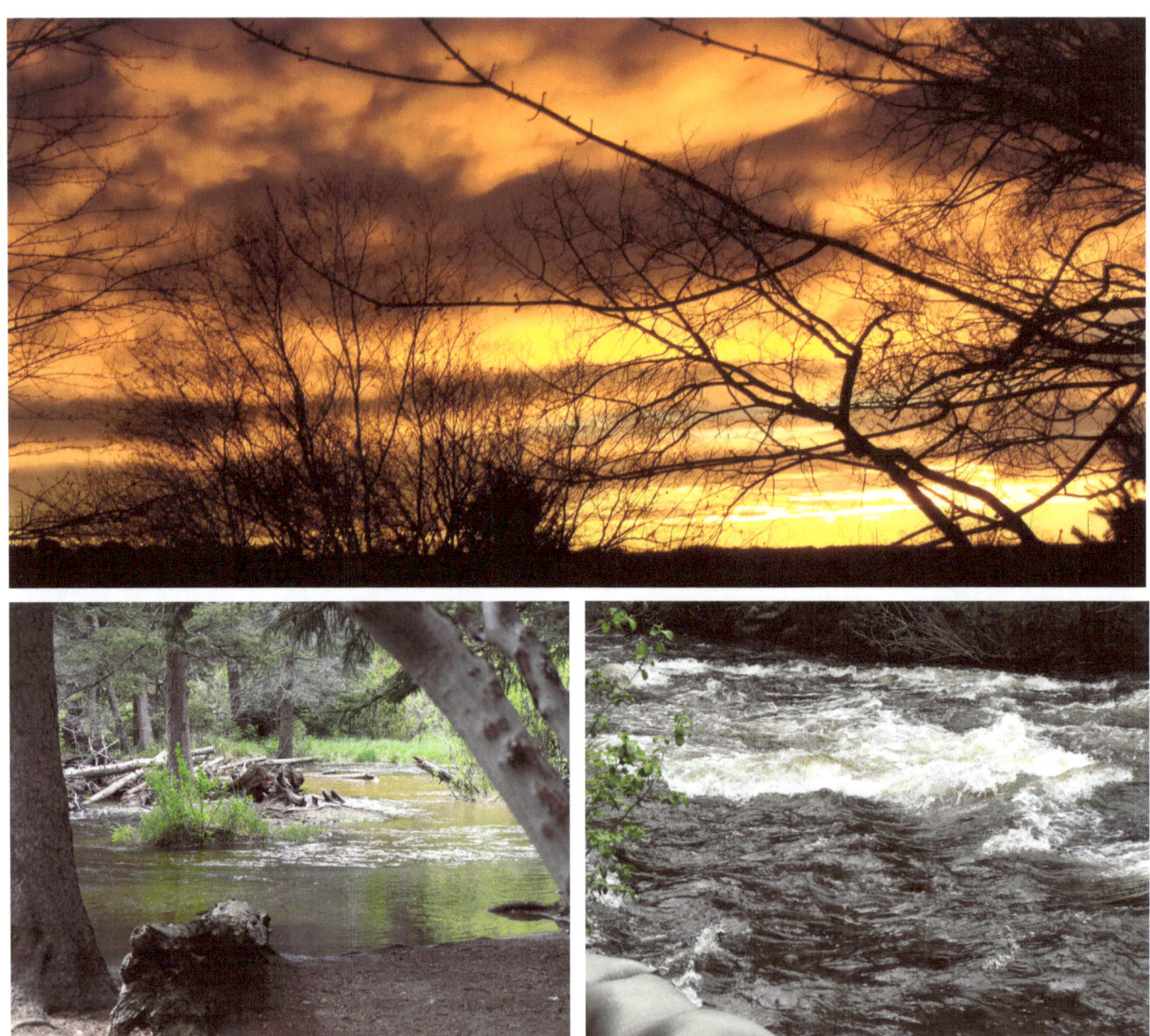

A Time ...

To give thanks. *November* is a month to focus on the concept of thanksgiving. Does the Bible really say to give thanks in all circumstances? Surely, not in all circumstances:

* ❖ I've lost my job–my employer is downsizing

* ❖ The doctor gave me three months to live–he asked if I had a bucket list

* ❖ My home is nothing but rubble–the fire took everything

* ❖ My dog was run over by a car–that was my only family

* ❖ I have known nothing but abuse–I trust no one; I don't know love

* ❖ My spouse is gone—where do I go from here

* ❖ This is as good as my life gets–from here everything spirals downward

* ❖ My whole town is swept away by the hurricane–my life is gone

* ❖ I have lost my only child–I have nothing left for which to live

* ❖ My home and farm are completely destroyed by the flood— my livelihood is spent

With the help of God, we can be thankful even when our **heavy** thoughts pull us downward. We can be thankful for His promises–even in very difficult occurrences. We have God's comfort and peace beyond all human understanding (John 14:27; John 16:33).

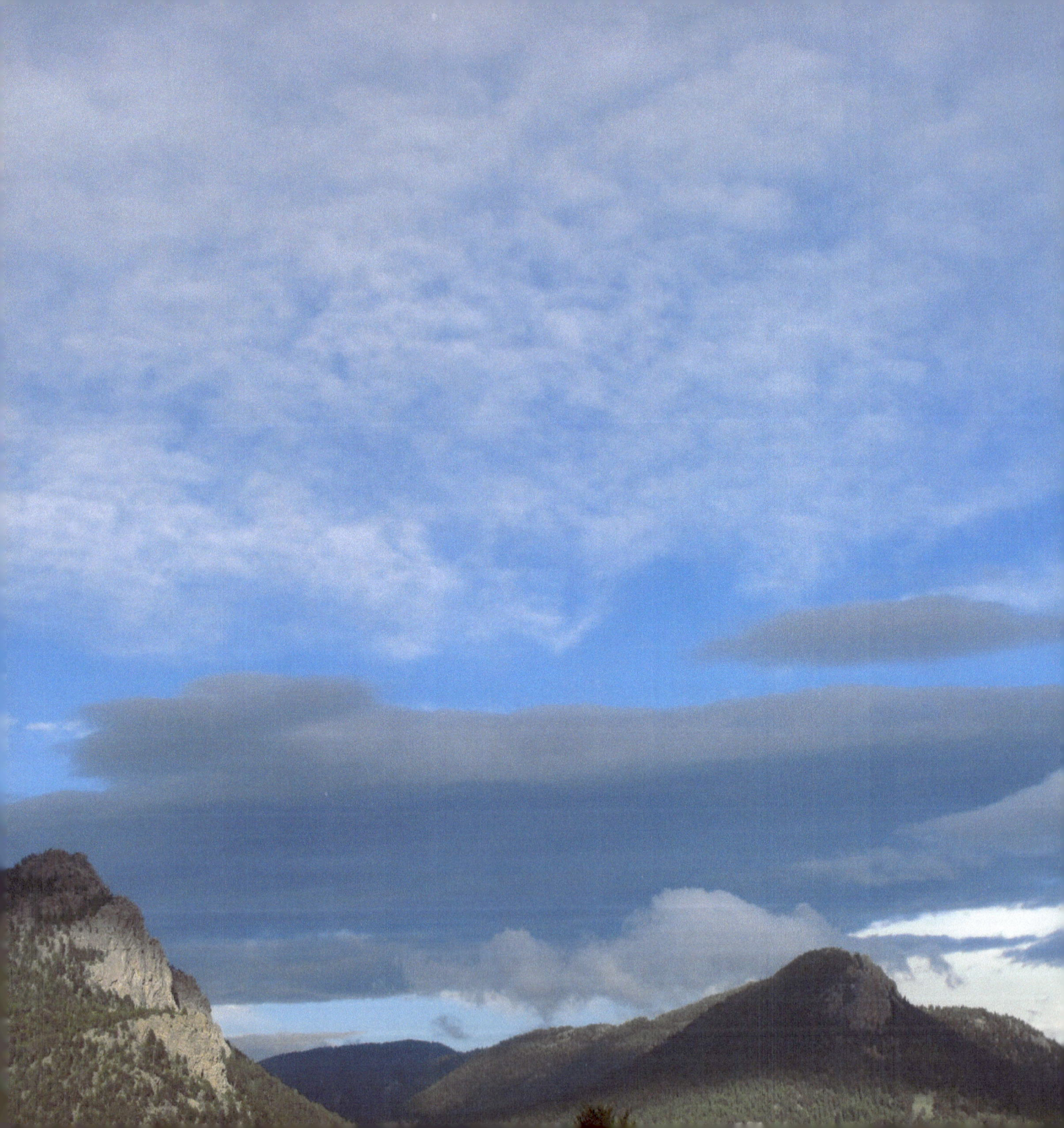

God's promises are true: "Your love, O Lord reaches to the heavens, Your faithfulness to the skies" (Psalm 36:5, NIV). "Never will I leave you; never will I forsake you" (Hebrews 13:5, NIV). "When you pass through the waters, I will be with you; and through the rivers, they shall not overflow you. When you walk through the fire, you shall not be burned, nor shall the flame scorch you" (Isaiah 43:2, NKJV).

When our hearts and minds are filled with God's promises and thanksgiving for those promises, we cannot but overflow to others and share why we can be joyful in such sorrowful times. We want to give to others the **happiness** we receive from God's Word:

"Blessed be the God and Father of our Lord Jesus Christ, the Father of mercies and God of all comfort, who comforts us in all our tribulation, that we may be able to comfort those who are in any trouble, with the comfort with which we ourselves are comforted by God" (2 Corinthians 1:3-4, NKJV).

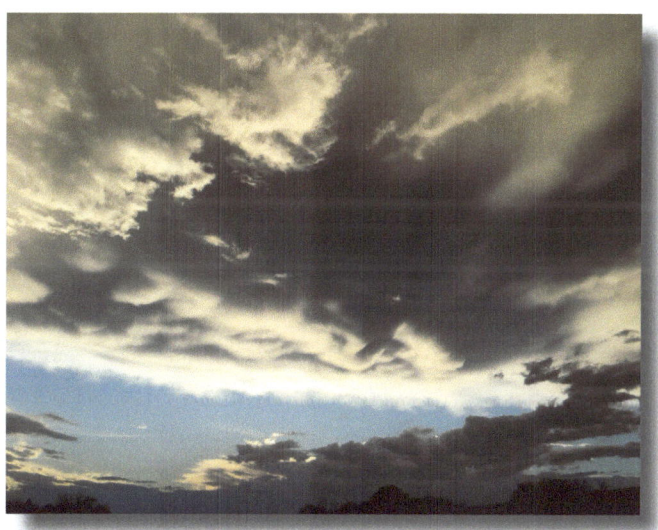

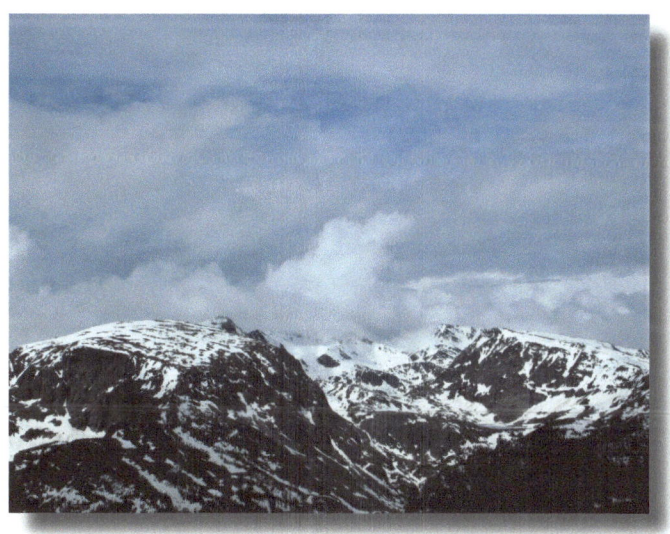

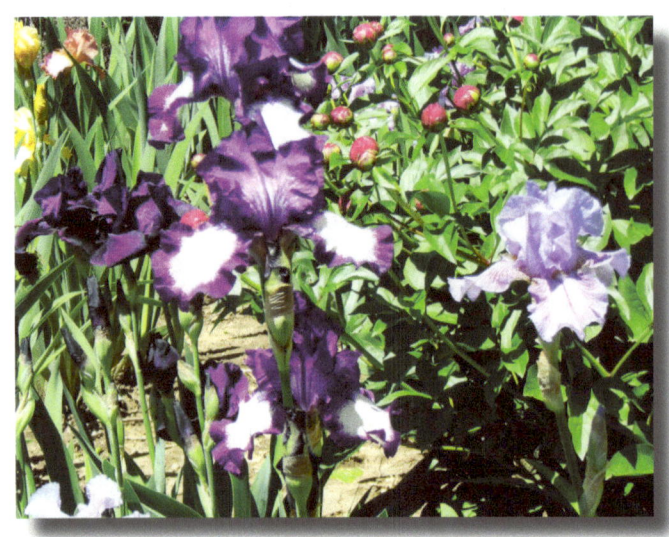

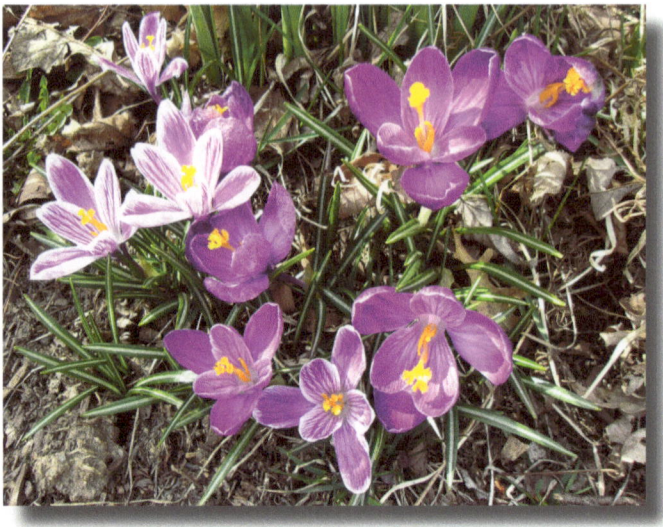

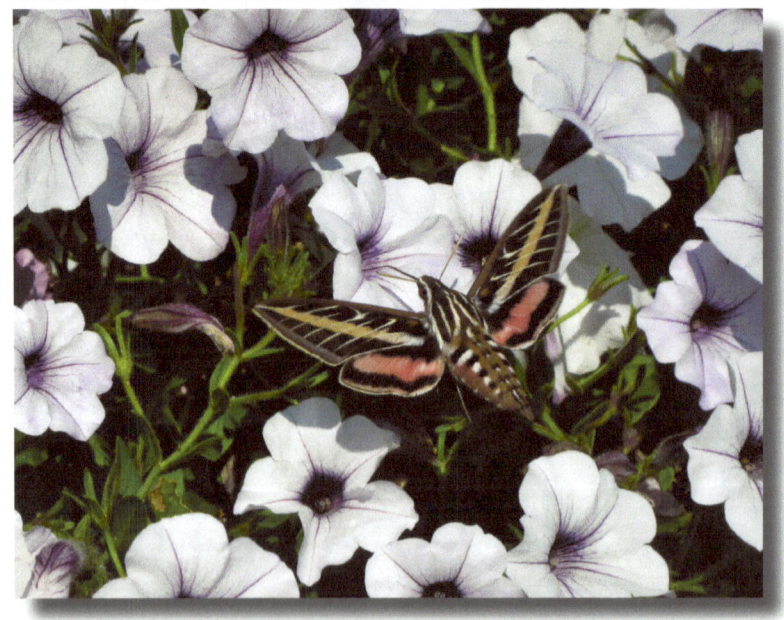

What a great time to be alive! We have a loving Father in heaven who welcomes us to snuggle up close to Him in order to share with Him all that is overflowing from our hearts.

The following words in a song summarize very well one of the greatest promises for which to be thankful: "Give thanks with a grateful heart, give thanks to the Holy One, give thanks because He's given Jesus Christ His Son."[1]

Because Jesus came into this world, hope remains when this world disappoints. God's promises continue unchanged.

"Oh, give thanks to the Lord, for He is good! For His mercy endures forever"
(1 Chronicles 16:34, Psalm 118:1, Psalm 136:1).

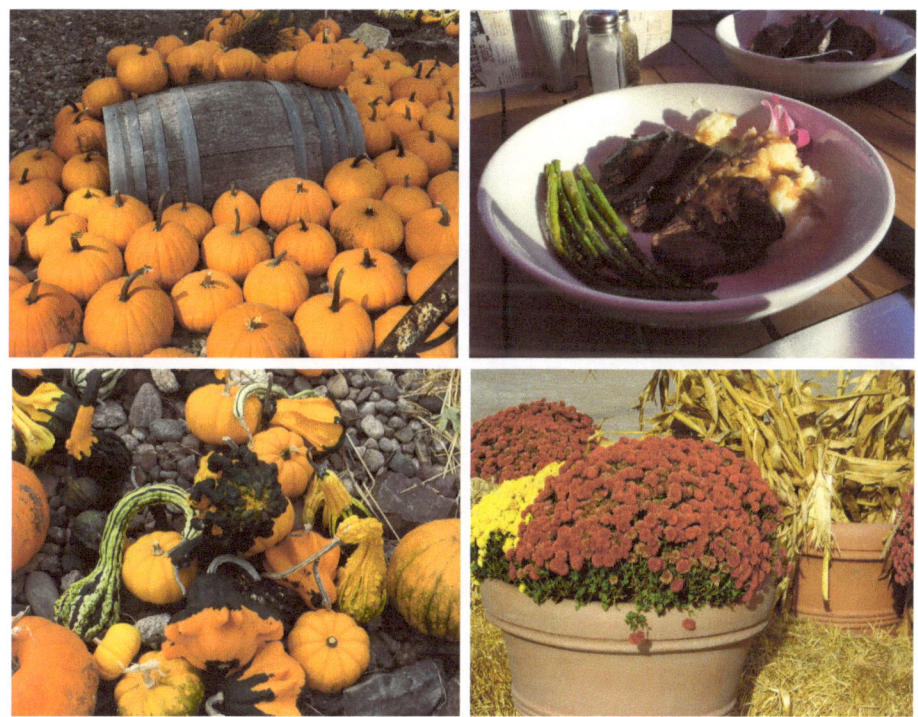

[1] *Give Thanks with a Grateful Heart*; Henry Smith (1978).

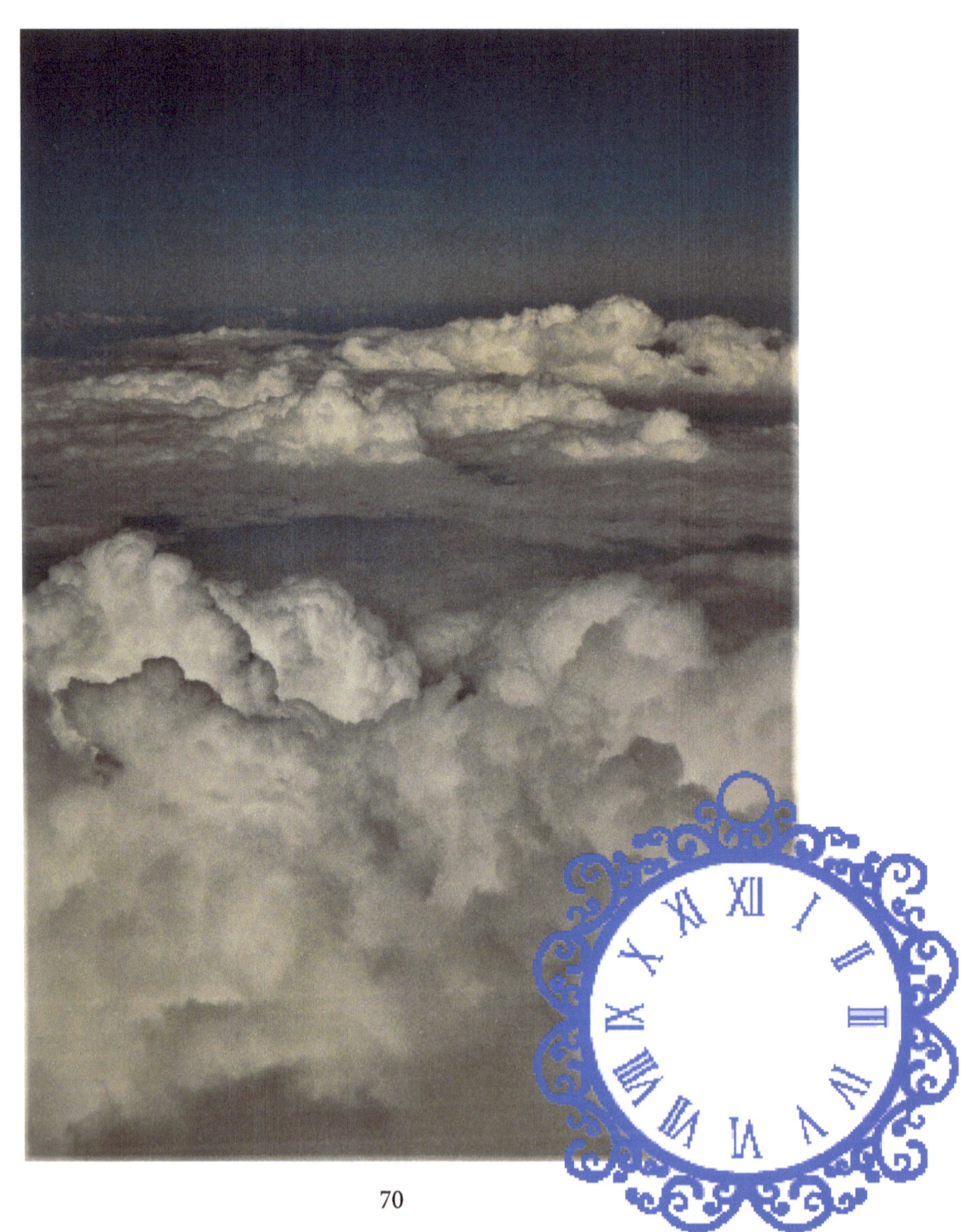

A Time ...

To grow. **December** in North America reveals days when sunlight hours grow shorter, and dark hours grow longer. The hours in a day remain constant, but activities may change slightly to accommodate for the loss of light. More activities are accomplished indoors.

One amazing occurrence from the past, however, happened extraordinarily outdoors. Shepherds in their usual manner watched their sheep by night to protect them from robbers or wild animals. Their outside activities were interrupted. "And an angel of the Lord suddenly stood before them, and the glory of the Lord shone around them; and they were terribly frightened" (Luke 2:9, NASB).

Although the shepherds were frightened, they grew more enlightened with each moment. They learned from the angel the following:

"Do not be afraid, for behold, I bring you good tidings of great joy which will be to all people. For there is born to you this day in the city of David a Savior, who is Christ the Lord. And this will be the sign to you: You will find a Babe wrapped in swaddling cloths, lying in a manger" (Luke 2:10-12, NKJV).

With a message on their tongue, they shared what they heard and saw. The news grew and spread to all who would hear.

Many years have passed since that tiny baby stirred in Bethlehem. Because that baby known as Jesus was the Son of God, whoever believes in Him should not perish but have everlasting life (John 3:16).

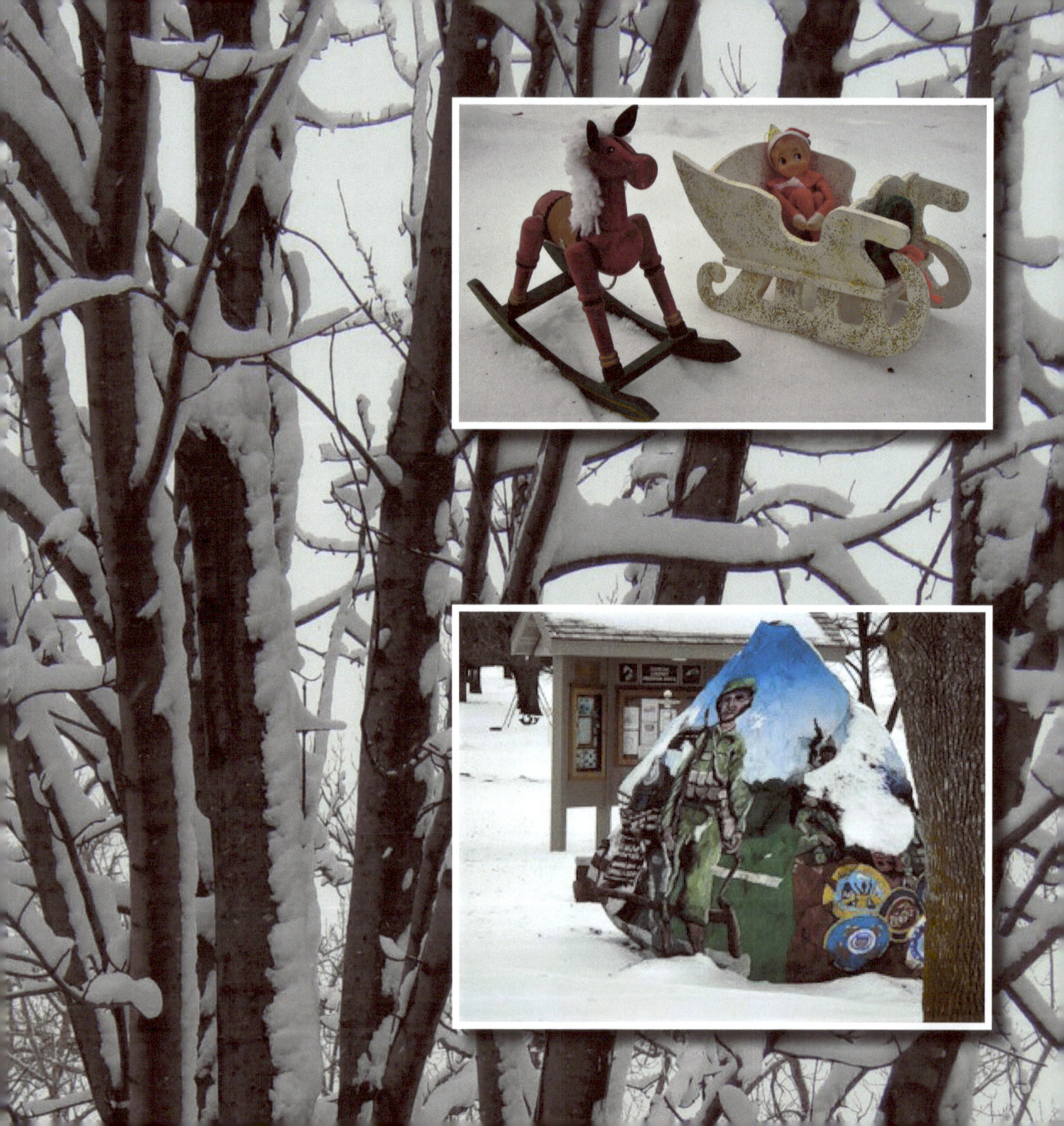

Although the number of lives lost in the name of freedom grows, the price of one life in particular, Jesus Christ, is beyond all measure. Because He submitted to death but then overcame death by rising to life again, we have only to believe and receive Him into our heart to inherit the life eternal he desires for us. What joy knowing that Jesus gives us freedom from sin, death, and the power of Satan.

Honing our storytelling skills of this wonderful news from the Bible, as well as real life stories from family and friends (to keep alive the appreciation of this God-given freedom) may be one of those precious threads that intertwine generations.

As we await the celebration of our Savior's birth, let us grow in anticipation of a new eternal home with the One who loves beyond all human measure and understanding. Let the love of Jesus spread. **Let it grow, let it grow, let it grow!**

Merry Christmas!

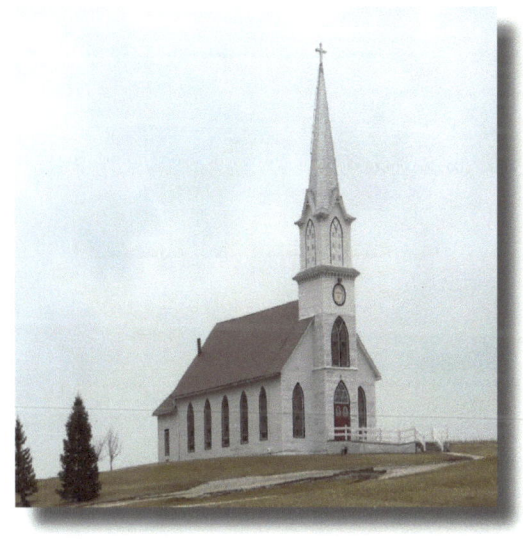
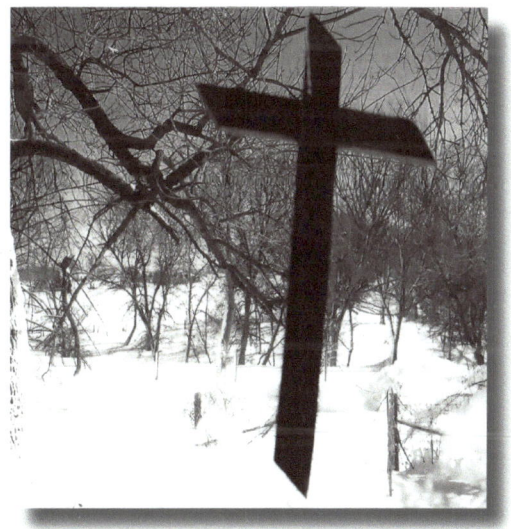

Sights of Significance

Notes

Notes

www.ingramcontent.com/pod-product-compliance
Lightning Source LLC
Chambersburg PA
CBHW050737180526
45159CB00003B/1257